holier than thou

JACKIE HILL PERRY

holier than thou

HOW GOD'S HOLINESS HELPS US TRUST HIM

FOREWORD *by* CHARLIE DATES

B&H
PUBLISHING
NASHVILLE, TENNESSEE

To my children, Eden, Autumn, and Sage.

This work wasn't written for you but around you. While you played, I studied and thought deeply about the nature of God. While you were away at school or in your rooms, I wrote as much of it as I could. At times you interrupted me with the want to tell me something or show me anything, and whenever you did, I thought to myself, *This is holy, too.* There is a child-like purity in the way you look to me for most things.

I pray that what is written next is what you've seen me obey so that when each of you is old enough to read Mommy's words and understand the holy God it explains, that if and when you make the decision to be like Mommy, my example actually means you will be more like God.

Acknowledgments

Preston, Mother, and Dana, Thank you
Austin, Devin, and Ashley, Thank you
Father, Son, and Spirit, Thank You

Contents

foreword

DEEP INSIGHTS INTO THE character of God don't come without great trial. Ask Moses. He spent the better part of forty years in ignominy until he met God at that burning bush. His life in the wilderness was more of a personal and professional desert than it was an address in the backwoods of desolation. Some of the best revelation about God, however, came at the expense of his personal wasteland.

Ask Ruth. A Moabite bereft of kinsmen, pelted on the fringes of sixth-century womanhood, but determined to see providence run its course. Her story and lineage bequeath to us pieces of the mystery of God on the canvass of her struggle.

Nobody experiences revelation without some great cost. Sometimes, the tariff is our own transgression. Ask David. Somewhere between Bathsheba and Absalom, his life became the studio for melodies from heaven. Much of the godly music we sing today hearkens from his trumpet of tribulation.

Ask Jackie. The book you hold in your hand was forged through time and trial. Jackie paid to write this book. Something of her weariness leaks through the ink on these pages. None of us come to love God deeply, to see Him clearly without first having an awakening to our internal depravity which can lead to a fuller appreciation of God's holiness. Something of the richness of her treasures found hide here in plain sight.

Every era needs its own prophet of holiness; a kind of living invitation to marvel in the beauty of God's holiness, and in the holiness of His beauty. It's the last part that grabs me: the holiness of His beauty. Our culture is bedazzled with images of fleeting majesty. We are so easily let down. The glisten of gold from Wall Street to Main Street bids anew on each passing generation. Sephora and Mac do their best to hide the spots and wrinkles of our worn countenances. Fame and influence beckon our singular devotion for their possession. We humans are on the hunt for a beauty that does not fade only to discover that it does fail.

While we need a prophet of holiness, now is not the time for empty moralism and pious irrelevancies. Neither of those is sufficient to sustain or satisfy. So many of our sermons and books, whether conservative or liberal, are but moral manifestos disguised as scholarly exegesis. We tire quickly of cold commands. We need a grander vision of God even if the window from which we see Him is small.

This book is a wide vision through a narrow window. I want to warn you, however. The complex enigma which is God's holiness is literally indescribable. Our best attempts are but anthropomorphic images, metaphors to decode mystery. Truth is, words will not do. God must be experienced. That, friend, is a frightening proposition. Few people, from Moses to D. L. Moody, could barely contain the awful joy after such an encounter. So, get ready. The words bound between these pages are like the rungs of a ladder to that vista where the subject is as glorious as the object.

I told Jackie that she is a gifted communicator, but I'm stunned that the readability is likewise so profound. Like an apologist and logician, she argues for our most reasonable faith. She has served her generation well. When A. W. Tozer wrote that "God is looking for men and women in whose hands His glory is safe," he must have been thinking about a captivated saint like Jackie.

I read this book and wanted more of God.

I poured over its pages with both interjection and applause.

I wasn't ready for the bliss that found me.

Here it is. Read it and weep for joy.

Dr. Charlie Dates, senior pastor of Progressive Baptist Church and an affiliate professor at Trinity Evangelical Divinity School and Baylor's George W. Truett Theological Seminary

Introduction

TONI MORRISON ONCE SAID, "If there's a book that you want to read, but it hasn't been written yet, then you must write it."[1] So here I am, writing.

Walk into a seminary, peruse an aisle, ask your pastor for his favorite, your friend for hers, your father for his, and they will all have a "holy" book to offer you. I've read so many of them at this point, and the shape of my soul, the stretch of my mind, and this work you hold is the proof. I honor the likes of G. E. Patterson, John Onwuchekwa, R. C. Sproul, A. W. Tozer, Stephen Charnock, and David Wells for how they helped me to think about the subject. I dignify gospel songs like "Nobody Greater," "Nobody Like You, Lord," and "Nobody Like Jesus" for putting melody to it. I remember my Aunt Merle, the first holy woman I knew. I know a halo when I see it because of her little brown self. She wore it always. That haloed woman, I honor too. These

---

[1] Ellen Brown, "Writing Is Third Career for Morrison," *Cincinnati Enquirer*, September 27, 1981.

influences have been good to me, but even with their help, I still had questions about the holy subject they introduced me to.

I don't remember the day I thought about it and if my coffee was iced or warm. What I know is that what I thought, and what I thought of, I wanted an answer for: "If God is holy, then He can't sin. If God can't sin, then He can't sin against me. If He can't sin against me, shouldn't that make Him the most trustworthy being there is?"

It's possible that I thought about people before this and the reasons why I don't trust *them*. People are incredibly problematic, to say the least. They're born into this place with bad blood and inconsistent intentions, and of course, this isn't what any of them (me included) was created to be. God made us to image Himself. To exist in the world in such a way that when observed, whoever looked at us could accurately imagine God. But when you add in an inquisitive demon, a woman deceived, a man's forbidden bite, and God's law broken because of it, what you don't have left is native goodness. You have the generational inheritance of everything unholy, which makes everyone with it unlike God. The same impulse that lifted Cain's hand and necessitated the crying voice of his own brother's blood is within every person alive. This, I believe, is the root of every reason we don't trust people. We know that if a person is a sinner, then bad behavior is always a possibility and God forbid we get too close and they make an Abel out of us. We distrust as protection (wisely at times) from the lift of their hand and the cry of our own blood. Whether the killing is verbal, emotional, or physical, we keep ourselves from the potential of all three because we've seen our own sinful nature and have experienced enough sins against us to know that sinners aren't trustworthy.

What about God, though? Is He as negligent as everyone else? Is He a being with the potential to be as bad as us? As Cain and his father, the first sinner? If not, why do we treat Him like we do all the others? Is it that we've mistaken the Second Adam for the first and have thought of Him as a "better" version of ourselves? Is it that we think His goodness, though great, isn't consistent? Or that His commands are true only when they don't hurt? As if when His instruction costs you an arm, leg, or life, then He must be lying? What I am trying to get at is that somewhere lurking at the bottom of our unbelief is the thought that God isn't holy. One goal of this work you're holding is to prove that "if" doesn't belong in front of "God is holy." Since He is, as the following chapters will show, He can and should be trusted.

According to the writer of Hebrews, without faith, it's impossible to please God (Heb. 11:6). So then, faith must always be a part of the discussion of how we're to interact with Him. Without it, we are damnable. With it, we move mountains. Without it, we are an unstable sea, having two minds in one body. With it, we are a home, built on a rock. When the winds come to throw their weight against the frame, it—or should I say *we*—will not break. It makes sense why of all the things the serpent could come for, it is our faith he attacks most. By walking through the Scriptures, we will see the Holy God as He is so that we can place our faith in who He has revealed Himself to be. Faith isn't optional in this case. We must trust God like our life depends on it because it does.

From this faith in God, fruit grows. Holiness shows up in us, making us trustworthy, honest, self-controlled, gentle, wise, pure, and more. As obvious as it seems, our own efforts at sanctification are not always framed in this way—that faith in Christ and who He has revealed God to be precedes holiness. The call to a holy life has commonly presented God's hatred of sin as the primary incentive of purity in contrast to exalting God Himself as the reason. I was raised under that technique. Where the preacher stood erect behind the pulpit to tell me the truth. That without holiness, no man would see the Lord. That as a sinner, God would do me like He did Sodom, scaring me and all the other kids in my youth group into pseudo-sanctity. The discernible problem is twofold: I wasn't provided with a vision of the Holy God that explained His infinite worth, denying me the joy of what happens when God Himself is the incentive for repentance. Nor was I handed a shovel and encouraged to dig beneath my sins and see what was underneath so as to give me context for why I sinned as I did.

The soil from which all sin grows is unbelief. We sin because it is our nature to do so, but it's not as if we always sin unintentionally, like depraved robots without the ability to behave according to reason. We are thoughtful with our rebellion. There is a level of reasoning within us when we decide which golden calf we'll love on any given day. With that said, the foundation of our idolatry, the sin begetting all others, is a specific belief about God. Our perverse sexual ethics, wild tongue, religious superiority, dark thoughts, legalistic posture, mean ways, impatient moods, greedy antics, intellectual arrogance, and rebellious tendencies come out of what we believe about the living God. I'm not referring to the temptation of these acts, but to the practice. We do one or all of the above when we have made the decision not to believe, trust, acknowledge, or depend on who God has revealed Himself as in some way.

Let's take the "Rich Young Ruler," for example, who comes to Jesus with a necessary question: "What must I do to inherit eternal life?" (Mark 10:17–22; Matt. 19:16–22; Luke 18:18–23). There's something admirable about the nameless ruler that he'd want to know how to live forever, but notice how he addresses the One who knew. He calls Jesus "good teacher." Ignoring "teacher," Jesus pokes at his superficial application of "good." "Why do you call me good? No one is good except God alone." The implication is obvious. The ruler has come with a question for a teacher he considers good but not God. This belief is so authentic to the ruler that he's sincere when speaking to the incarnate God, who alone is good, when he says he's kept His law, as if to say that he is *good* too. What he thinks of Jesus drives how he thinks of himself, which sets the stage for his refusal to sell everything he has so that Jesus could be his ultimate treasure. If Jesus is just good but not God, then the command to follow Him is optional. Not only that, if Jesus is just good but not God, then technically, He isn't any *better* than what the ruler had much of. Why give up good things for a smart man unless the truth is that this man is God too and thus better than every good thing there is? To choose such a truth would make surrender a matter of exchanging broken cisterns for living water, the lot of the blessed ones who hunger and thirst, who will be filled because they believed about God what He said of Himself (Ps. 107:9; Jer. 2:13; Matt. 5:6). Can you see that just like the young ruler, what we believe about God will determine how we behave?

If that is the case, I suspect that many of the methods and messages related to holiness may actually be encouraging the opposite, leading to an earth-grown morality rather than a heaven-sent righteousness. If and when holiness is prescribed in a way that doesn't involve addressing the underlying belief systems leading to sin, we're potentially fumbling the ball. Let's say that a person decided to go to somebody's church, sit in their pew, sing their songs, then a sermon about holiness goes forth. In it they hear things like, "Take up your cross and die daily." And "You cannot serve God and money." What good does it do the hearer if they believe God is a liar? They disobey because they don't believe Jesus has life in Himself, real life, better than any superficial life the world offers. If this isn't brought to the surface, will they trust His call to die or will they imagine that life is just fine without Him? What if there is no talk of God's supreme value—how, as God, He is better than everything that exists? Without it, what incentive is there to eliminate a lesser master in exchange for a good One? What motivation is there to believe that God is more faithful than their income? We have supposed that the way to help people be holy is to just tell them to "stop sinning," when in fact, lasting transformation is a spiritual consequence of "beholding the glory of the Lord" (2 Cor. 3:18).

That's why we're here: to behold. To set our sights on a higher love. To see who Adam hid from, who the psalmists sang to, who the prophets spoke for, who the disciples walked with, and who Jesus made known. I know that "holy" comes with a world of baggage. We think of it and imagine boredom incarnated. A smile-less woman. An uptight man who looks as if he's never loved anything at all. From our experience with the religious and how it makes some people mean as a bull, we may think holiness looks like them. Distant, cold, knowledgeable of the Scriptures and ignorant of the heart. Whether it is joyless or callous, neither describes God.

God's holiness is essential to His nature and fundamental to His being. His holiness is what makes Him good, and loving, and kind, and faithful. Without holiness, God wouldn't be beautiful, and so because of it, He is eternally attractive. Think about the opposite of it being present in Him and you may see my point. If He were sovereign, but wicked, with no inner righteousness to restrain His hand, I wouldn't be surprised if the world was no more. If He had all power without love, our refusal to love Him back would result in cosmic abuse or maybe a million more floods with no rainbow to promise His relent. If He were an unholy

God, what would salvation even mean? What is deliverance to a self-centered "savior"? Thankfully, our God is incomprehensibly holy and therefore completely beautiful in all of His ways and works. This is why we are invited to worship Him as such, and in so doing, we become just as beautiful as He is.

What's coming after this is simple. I'm writing what I've wanted to read. The words that explain the beauty of God in His holiness have already been written to us through the inspired words of Scripture, so know that I'm not going to say anything new. I'm just being faithful to what I believe Scripture has described which I haven't heard enough of. So if there is anything I want this work to do, it's to show you God. There is no one greater. No one better. No one worthy of our entire selves, and I believe that as you see Him as He is, you'll want to be just like Him too.

Holy.

Chapter 1

Holy, Holy, Holy

IMAGINE YOURSELF AS AN Israelite. Egypt and its gods are a recent memory. There are fifty days between you and the sea that divided itself in half so you could walk on dry ground. In the desert now, you're told that in three days, you're going to meet God. God? Yes, God. You've never seen His face, but you can suspect how He might be when you remember His ways. You remember the day when the water turned red and the river bled out. When all of the dust beneath your feet began to crawl. When one morning, the wind blew, bringing with it a swarm of locusts so large they covered the sun, making everything black and eating everything green. On the last night, right in the middle of it, you heard what sounded like a communal sadness. You remember how afraid you were that the sorrow down the street was on its way to your home—a traveling grief? Desperate to know if the blood on your door kept your firstborn from a sovereign death, you put your face to theirs until you felt breath. The blood worked.

Now the day has come for you and the rest of Israel to meet God for yourselves. It's morning, and in your tent, you watch as shadows grow all around you. The sun isn't shining as bright as it typically does, and you wonder why. As you converse with your own curiosity, what sounds like thunder reaches into the space around you. You can't tell if it's at the same time or not, but one second after the noise, lightning scatters across the clouds like confetti on fire. There's no rain to accompany either, but there's a trumpet played by only God knows who that's loud enough for you and all of Israel to know the musician isn't human. Your hands shake. Your heart paces, back and forth. You look at your firstborn and remember to breathe.

You're at the bottom of the mountain now. Close enough to see it's wrapped in smoke. Far enough to stay alive. You follow your line of sight, past the bottom of it and the burning parts, all the way up to the top where smoke shoots out of the mountain's mouth and levitates into the clouds—the very same place the invisible trumpet player must've been located. Clearly discontent with the initial volume of his instrument, the sound of it gets louder and louder. As it plays, you get it now. You're realizing that you were delivered from Pharaoh in Egypt so you could meet the King in the desert. You're recognizing the difference between this God and the others. That unlike them, creation does this God's bidding and not the other way around. He seems to be above it and everyone. Different than Egypt's gods who were imagined into being. Those gods imaged their makers because they too were *made.* They too were immoral, expecting of Egypt a righteousness easy enough for any of Eve's children to keep. This God expects nothing less than an awful[1] obedience from you and everything else, and you know it. The plagues sit in the back of your mind as a reminder of what kind of King you're about to meet. One that can use rivers and bugs and reptiles and nature itself against you. Like your hands, the mountain shakes. Like your heart, it can't get still because now, finally, in the midst of the thunder smack, the fire-lit sky, and the trumpet blast, descending on the mountain in fire is God. If you didn't know it then, you know it now, that this God, this King, is holy.

> For you have not come to what may be touched,
> a blazing fire and darkness and gloom and a
> tempest and the sound of a trumpet and a
> voice whose words made the hearers beg that

---

[1] "Awful: filled with awe; deeply respectful or reverential" (*Merriam-Webster*).

no further messages be spoken to them. . . .
Indeed, so terrifying was the sight that Moses
said, "I tremble with fear." . . . But you have
come to Mount Zion and to the city of the living
God . . . Therefore let us be grateful for receiving a kingdom that cannot be shaken, and thus
let us offer to God acceptable worship, with
reverence and awe, for our God is a consuming
fire. (Heb. 12:18–19, 21–22, 28–29)

God Is Holy

Israel saw with their eyes what we've come to know by
faith, that God is holy. To say that God is holy is to say that
God is God. All of God's ways, such as His moral purity
and how it sets Him apart from all that is perverse, untrue,
lawless, and unrighteous comes out of His being. No one
told or taught God how to be good; that is simply who He
is, and He can be no other way. As Stephen Charnock put
it, "God is good as he is God; and therefore good by himself and from himself, not by participation from another."[2]
It is His very nature to be righteous, as in right, as in

---

[2] Stephen Charnock, *Discourses upon the Existence and
Attributes of God*, volumes 1–2 (New York: Robert Carter &
Brothers, 1874), 221.

conforming to a set standard of morality, the standard being Himself. We are only good insofar as we are like God, so then, any attempt to be holy is an attempt to be like God. Simply put, the two are inseparable, holiness and God's being, that is.

There are times when our conversations around the holiness of God make it seem as if holiness is a *part* or *piece* of God. That God moves in between attributes when deciding how to be. That one day, He chooses to be loving. Another day, He chooses to be vengeful. That if God were a sweet potato pie, holiness is one slice of it that's set aside from the others. On one plate is holiness; on another plate is love. However, holiness is not an aspect of God; holy is who He is through and through. His attributes are never at odds with one another, nor do they switch places depending on God's mood; they are *Him.* "God *is* his attributes. That means, all that is in God simply is God."[3] When God loves, it is a holy love. When God reveals Himself as judge, pouring out His cup on the deserving, He has not ceased to be loving, or holy either. In all that He is and all that He does, He is always Himself.

---

[3] Matthew Barrett's essay, "Divine Simplicity," https://www.thegospelcoalition.org/essay/divine-simplicity/.

Even now, I hope you're beginning to see the glory of God. I don't mean that hypothetically either. Since holiness is essential to God, shining through all that He is and whatever He does, it means that there has never been or will ever be a time when God is not God. To say it another way, there will never come a day when God ceases to be holy; if that were possible, it would be the day He ceased to be God. Knowing that as an absolute and unmovable truth colors everything we understand about God's ways and works.

Holiness Revealed in Creation

In creation, He was holy. Man was made to image His righteousness, and all the other things like the sky, the ground underneath it, and the animals on it were judged as good by God. When He applies the word to anything, He is telling the truth, for if anybody knows how to use it the right way it would be Him. The rich young ruler put "good" in his address to Jesus, to which Jesus asked him *why*. Why call Him good if only God is? This wasn't a denial of He whose divinity was veiled. It was to say that the attribution of good as it related to Jesus was to tell the truth about who He really was. If good, then God. If God, then good. A good God makes good things. Good? All of the time.

Holiness Revealed in the Fall

After the two goodie-two-shoes took them off to place their feet on unholy ground, the bad things came. With sin came judgment. As judge, God is holy still. Some finite folk can't seem to reconcile this, that judgment is a *good (holy)* thing. I'm not omniscient in any way. I'm completely blind to the motives that move them to make up things about what should or shouldn't be true about the Holy One, but if I had to guess, I'd say their lack of applause for God's justice comes out of their desire for Him to be like them: unrighteous. "It is too common for men to fancy God not as he is but as they would have him; strip him of his excellency for their own security."[4] If they had it their way, the guilty could go about life unpunished, freed from judgment as underneath the stayed gavel of God. The problem with that is this: to want God to withhold justice is to want God to make Himself an abomination. "He who justifies the wicked and he who condemns the righteous are both alike an abomination to the LORD" (Prov. 17:15). This would be for Him to become a loathsome, detestable being, more like Satan than Himself. It's an impossible ask and border-line blasphemous, so as God is, He will remain. Holy and

---

[4] Charnock, *Discourses upon the Existence and Attributes of God*, 172.

therefore just. "But the LORD of hosts is exalted in justice, and the Holy God shows himself holy in righteousness" (Isa. 5:16).

Holiness Revealed in Redemption

In the redemption of souls, God is holy. Out of His righteousness, God gave a law. At first, it was to not eat. If obeyed by faith in the purity and worth of the lawgiver, the two garden misfits would've continued in His love. Refusing this, their nature was eventually inherited by every generation. One that loves the dark more than the Son. Born like them too, Israel was provided with a written law. A set of commands, good ones in fact, that imaged God in its insistence to do right by Him and others. None of them saw such behavior as a good thing, of course. Who *wants* to love God above all things when there are so many deficient alternatives for which to place our affections? The gods they collected were an incomplete thing. Like cisterns broken all up, wasting water all over the place. These lesser gods were unable to make anyone who trusts in them whole; neither could they transcend their created nature if ever they were asked to deliver. But, Israel loved their idols still, and so do we.

As is expected of God, then, judgment must come down on the heads of those with a hesitant "yes, Lord."

His righteousness will not allow the guilty to go unpunished. Scary, to fall into the hands of the living God, until we believe in the One who did so in our place. The cross reveals God's holiness in how the sinless Son was judged on behalf of sinful people so that when God justifies the guilty, He does so without compromising His righteousness. The Holy Spirit is then sent to fill and sanctify us as a means of restoring our divine resemblance, helping us to wear the right clothes and two good shoes, wherein we "put on the new self, created after the likeness of God in true righteousness and holiness" (Eph. 4:24). From the beginning with creation, in our redemption and eventual glorification, God's holiness is revealed.

Holy, Holy, Holy

To go deeper into what Scripture means when it testifies that God is holy, let's glean from Isaiah's vision of Him. In the sixth chapter of the book titled after the prophet's name, written in it is the song of the seraphim. About God they say to one another, "Holy, holy, holy is the LORD of hosts; the whole earth is full of his glory!" (v. 3). Notice the word used thrice. It isn't "love, love, love" or "good, good, good" but "holy, holy, holy."

Why is that important? Well, in Hebrew language and literature, the use of repetition was common practice.

Jesus used it often by beginning his lessons with the words "Truly, truly." By this, His listeners knew that all that was to follow was significant and true. Rarely in Scripture do you see this literary device used to the third degree; never do you see it used to the third degree to address an attribute of God except here in Isaiah and in Revelation 4:8 ("Holy, holy, holy is the Lord God Almighty"). With all three "holys," the seraphim are emphasizing the absolute, unalterable, essential, and total holiness of God.

To say that God is holy, holy, holy is to say that God is *most* holy. He is totally holy. Completely holy. Unwaveringly holy. Utterly holy. If you're in need of more words to describe the emphatic nature of God's holiness, the thesaurus offers up these in addition to the word *most*: *greater, highest, utmost, uttermost*. So then, God's holiness is great. The highest holy. He is holy to the uttermost. The Lord is holy beyond comparison for His holiness is not a derivative of some other source. His holiness is intrinsic to His nature as God. It's as essential to Him as creaturely dependence is to us. Of all the songs to sing to one another, of all the divine attributes worth praising God for, Isaiah saw the seraphim make melody around the supreme holiness of God.

Like trees, words have roots. Dig underneath the letters' soil and you'll discover its definition. The root word of "holy" means "to cut" or "to separate." When applied to everything outside of God, whatever is holy is whatever is set apart unto and for God. For example, God sanctified the Sabbath day, setting it apart from all other days as one in which His people were to rest in Him. That's why the Sabbath is called holy throughout the Old Testament. God separated it; He set it apart. In another example, the ground on which Moses stood was called holy, not because the dirt was divine but because the presence of the Holy One sanctified it, setting it apart from all other ground (Exod. 3:5).

There's a sermon by the great Tony Evans[5] in which he uses an illustration involving dishes to make sense of the term "holy." In his home, and in most homes really, there are two *types* of dishes. There are the regular dishes. The ones you corner off with French fries and squirt with ketchup. Those dishes that contain the average meal, on normal days, for your ordinary and unimpressive breakfast, lunch, and dinner. Some of them are chipped, maybe even cracked, and if they are, you don't whine over their disposal because they were never made to be special anyway.

Then there is another type of dish. These dishes don't even see the light of day until a tall green tree with

---

[5] Tony Evans sermon, "The Secret to Powerful Prayer," (September 15, 2019), https://www.youtube.com/watch?v=EVkC-zzubWY.

multi-colored lights flicker them onto the dining table. Something significant has to be happening under the roof to make their use a necessity. And when all is normal again, the candles have been blown out, the wrapping paper has been scattered and collected, the guests have finally gotten up from the table, these dishes, after being cleaned, aren't placed in the cabinets with the French fry and ketchup plates. Those are too typical and regular for their company. They're placed in an entirely different cabinet that may be in an entirely different room, separated from everything unlike them because there is nothing in the house like them. They are set apart, unique, different, other, distinct, cut off from what's considered common. To put it metaphorically, these dishes are "holy."

So to say of God that He is holy is to identify His position as a being that is set apart. From what or who is God separated from though? Holy people and things are holy only if they are separated unto God, but who is God set apart from? The answer is simple. God is unique, different, other, and distinct from everything that exists.

Moving backward to the beginning of the sixth chapter of Isaiah, what the seraphim say about God is observed by Isaiah. He says, "In the year that King Uzziah died I saw the Lord sitting upon a throne, high and lifted up; and the train of his robe filled the temple" (v. 1). First of all, it is when Uzziah dies, as in "gives up the ghost," that Isaiah sees God. Which is to say that though Uzziah is dead, God is alive. This may seem like an obvious truth that doesn't have much to do with holiness, but you are missing the point if you thought that for yourself. God isn't holy simply because He's alive. If that were the case, anybody with breath could be classified as holy. God is holy because God has *always* been alive, and after every king, person, plant, star, or moon passes away, He will still *be.* Even though all life begins with God, with God, there is no beginning. Another way to say it is that God is *self-existent.* He exists because He exists. He needs no one but Himself to *be;* therefore He always has and will always *be.*

Now, compare God to everything and tell me what you see. What I hope you noticed is that everything that exists has a beginning, is a derivative, is contingent upon something else for its life. Paul describes our lot as creatures, pointing to how it's only in God that we "live and move and have our being" (Acts 17:28). Can the same be said about God? Of course not. This is what is referred to as God's *transcendence.* It means that God is totally unique from everything there is. God doesn't exist and cannot exist in the same way as we do or anything for that matter; setting Him apart from all creation as a being that is distinct from it: holy. So, in this, we see that God's holiness is about moral purity, yes, and it's also about transcendent, self-existing otherness. It's about being totally right *and* eternally existent. Which, of course, only God is.

Isaiah sees the living God and calls Him "King, the LORD of Armies" (6:5 CSB). If the term "lord" was said of another, it wouldn't necessarily mean the person was holy. Such as Abraham who was called "lord" by Sarah, signifying the authority he holds as her husband. Or an owner of land, who in one case was called "the man, *the lord* of the land" who "spoke roughly to us and took us to be spies of the land" (Gen. 42:30, emphasis added). "Lord" in these cases convey a sense of "ownership" or "rights" one has over something. What makes the Lord as Isaiah sees Him different from that of Abraham is that as Sarah's husband, there's a covenantal ownership at play, where she is his and he is hers (1 Cor. 7:4), but Abraham could never claim sovereign authority over his wife or any other human being for that matter. He cannot treat her as if she existed because of him or that her life and being was ultimately dependent on him. The Lord being praised as holy is so because the titles "King" and "Lord of Armies" imply that He isn't merely an owner of something; He is the owner of everything—He is King of all the earth and ruler of the forces of heaven, too. Not with a few rights for which He has claim but with irrevocable rights over all that was made because all that was made was by His hand, for His glory. He is Lord because He is King and Creator. From Him came all things, the heavens and the earth of course. The world is His, with it are the hills, on it are the cattle that know Him as maker: "For every beast of the forest is mine, the cattle on a thousand hills. I know all the birds of the hills, and all that moves in the field is mine" (Ps. 50:10–11). God is Lord over the heavens, the earth that holds us, and Lord of the body to which we try our hardest to keep to ourselves. "The body is not meant for sexual immorality, *but for the Lord . . .*" (1 Cor. 6:13, emphasis added). With the Lord, there is a sovereign rule befitting Him as Master of all and servant of none.

Uzziah's authority over the small piece of the world that God allowed him to govern was limited in scope and time. Judah, with its millions of folks, was but dust compared to the universe to which God is Lord. His reign, Uzziah's that is, was all of fifty-two years. That's no petty amount of turned clocks, but it doesn't compare to the eternity for which God will always reign. He is the King of kings and so much more, "For the LORD your God is God of gods and Lord of lords, the great, the mighty, and the awesome God . . ." (Deut. 10:17). No being exists as sovereign over all but God—holy.

The Holy God is alive and well, as King of all who sits in a special way. The state of God's throne is one that is seen as "high and lifted up" (Isa. 6:1). You might think the mention of this is about altitude, and it might be in one way, but it's not simply that of geographical position but of preeminence. Height equivocates to the status of supreme. It speaks to the excellence of His being. God is high and lifted up because God is superior over all. He is infinitely valuable because He alone is God. He is "the One who is high and lifted up, who inhabits eternity, whose name is Holy . . ." (Isa. 57:15). We fancy the earth to be something special and it is because God made it that way, but even with all of its derived glory and perceived value, to God it is like a piece of furniture on which He places His feet. He said it Himself, "the earth is my footstool" (Isa. 66:1).

In other words, God rules with power He doesn't have to borrow. Upholding the world's orbit and the sun's heat with a strength Samson knew not of. He is majestic, a King with no equal. Every throne below Him is minuscule and without comparison. His ways are high and *higher* than ours because He is. He is the Most High, as in, He is exalted over everything that is because everything that is, might be good, but they will never be God. Everything wonderful that you have ever known—love, food, sex, laughter, friends, parents, children, sleep, work, money, you name it—can't compete with the beauty of God. The Most High calls Himself the Holy One and asks: "To whom then will you compare me, that I should be like him?" (Isa. 40:25). No one, Lord—holy.

If the singing wasn't enough for the prophet to bear, the sight of God, the robe's train claiming every inch, with nowhere to go and no strength to move, the foundations shook (v. 4). As the temple shivered without a breeze, Isaiah didn't praise. He knew the right things to say, true things. That before Him was "the LORD of hosts" (6:3) and the "Mighty One of Israel" (1:24). He could've invited himself into the seraphim's song as they called to one another about the King, their holy hymn. He decided against it, choosing instead to make his first word a familiar one: "Woe."

"Woe is me! For I am lost; for I am a man of unclean lips, and I dwell in the midst of a people of unclean lips; for my eyes have seen the King, the LORD of hosts!" (6:5). After seeing the holy God, Isaiah then saw himself. What he knew instantly was that between him and God, only one was truly holy. In the presence of the Lord, his guilt was obvious, his sins were bright, uncovered, exposed, broadcasted without a screen. Loud without a button to mute them or a finger to shush the noise. He confessed the defilement of his tongue which communicated the pollution native to his nature.

Of all the actions he could have taken, why do we see Isaiah confessing? Why are *words* what come out of him in such a moment? Because the mouth reveals what the heart holds. Jesus spoke to this when He said, "But what comes out of the mouth proceeds from the heart, and this defiles a person. For out of the heart come evil thoughts, murder, adultery, sexual immorality, theft, false witness, slander. These are what defile a person . . ." (Matt. 15:18–20a). To be a man of "unclean lips" was to be a man who is unclean, period.

Isn't it interesting how simply being in proximity to God creates a moral self-awareness in Isaiah and others?[6] That there is something about God that is so pure, even if unspoken, that when near Him, it becomes so plain that nothing is like Him, especially in terms of righteousness. It is not as though God *did* anything for Isaiah to be so terrified. God didn't even tell Isaiah He was holy at all; the seraphim did. God didn't move, come near, rise up or down; He simply *sat*, and that was enough for Isaiah to see his own wickedness. Just by being close, Isaiah's heart and its ways were impossibly noticeable. They were also discerned truthfully. He knew his lips were *unclean* and his community

---

[6] This is further explored in chapter 2, when we behold the interaction between Peter and Jesus.

with it. He let reality determine how he saw himself rather than using some pretty and undamnable word in exchange. He was a prophet who was more honorable in how he spoke and lived than that of the context to which he was called to prophesy against. If he'd stood there and within his mind, he put the nature of his speech next to them who called evil good and good evil, he might've thought himself pure. But before God—the One in whose mouth there is no deceit, whose perfections are unreachable, whose standard sits beyond the clouds and nowhere near close to any sky we could touch on our own—Isaiah knew he was a sinner.

The dramatic nature of Isaiah's clarity about his sinfulness highlights the moral excellence of the Lord who caused it. It's the intensity of what he learned about himself that proves that the high-and-lifted-up God is also *light*, as in, morally pure. "God is light, and in him is no darkness at all" (1 John 1:5). Light is often used as a metaphor for righteousness. In Proverbs, "But the path of the *righteous is like the light* of dawn" (Prov. 4:18, emphasis added). In Philippians, "Do all things without grumbling or disputing, that you may be *blameless and innocent*, children of God *without blemish* in the midst of a crooked and twisted generation, among whom you *shine as lights* in the world" (Phil. 2:14–15, emphasis added). Jesus is called "the light of the world" that if followed, He will give them "the light of life" (John 8:12).

Since God is light, God has no darkness. No evil within Him. No blemished heart or unclean hands. His thoughts are always good, His motives always pure. Tozer commenting on God's holiness says, "He is absolutely holy with an infinite, incomprehensible fullness of purity that is incapable of being other than it is."[7]

In the morning, when the sun stands up and shines on your part of the world, look toward it if you can and know that the Holy God is more brilliant than that. The radiant, incandescent light beaming forth from God's being has an illuminating effect. As it is with any source of light, it removes shadows, points to what was hiding behind it, tattle tales on the dark, and makes it acknowledge the secrets it couldn't keep. Anyone that loves evil hates light because of this. "For everyone who does wicked things hates the light and does not come to the light, lest his works should be exposed" (John 3:20). The contemporary man keeps his Bible closed in an attempt to quench its light. Others manufacture half-truths about God or refuse orthodoxy as a way to keep the Son out. Isaiah did neither, and he couldn't

---

[7] A. W. Tozer, *The Knowledge of the Holy* (New York: HarperCollins, 1961), 105.

even if he tried. When by the throne of the Holy One, the supreme virtue of His very being forced everything in Isaiah that didn't look like God to come out of hiding.

In the sixth chapter of Isaiah, we are provided with a vision of God that sets the table for our holy communion with Him. As we already saw, His holiness is both His transcendence and His moral purity. Both His incredible value over and above all things and His irrevocable commitment to the honoring of His name. A Lord who uses His power for good. A King without blemish. On a throne independent of time. He is high and lifted up and yet holy enough to humble Himself to death. Rising again to sit in His rightful place, where the creatures sing what is true about Him (Rev. 4:8). Through Him, we've received a kingdom that can't be shaken. Coming to Him, we have met with God. And we now know what we might not have known before. That this God and this King is holy.

Chapter 2

Holy, Holy, Holy: Moral Perfection

JESUS STEPPED INTO PETER'S boat as Himself. Not much and a whole lot had changed since King Uzziah's death. The Word had incarnated, for one. Born to a virgin, now human too, He'd aged to thirty. That day in Luke chapter 5, His clothing was much different than what the prophet saw. There was no robe or train filling the boat as it did the temple. The noise around wasn't angelic this time, but it was noisy all of the same. People chatted. Some murmured about the new prophet who had come to town doing things they'd never seen before. All of this was happening in front of a lake that had denied its fisherman any spoil the night before. This time, He was not in a temple with the seraphim's praise or speaking from a bush not consumed; the place where Jesus would sit and where God would speak now was a boat.

After He finished speaking, Jesus turned to Peter and told him to let down his nets (Luke 5:4). Peter had done this already, all night actually, with no fish to show for it. But he did what Jesus said even though it might've felt like a practice in futility. The once-empty net began to fill up with the same fish that were stubborn as all get-out before the sun came up. You would've thought they'd been called by name or led into the net by some invisible force. As the wind brought manna, the lake's current brought fish. So many of them were there, in fact, that the net began to break (v. 6). All of his experience with these fish, in that lake, in this boat, brought Peter to the conclusion that what was happening in that moment wasn't natural or even normal. And it was happening because the other man in his boat was more than a teacher, a prophet, and a healer. And even more than Mary's son, He was God.

"Depart from me, for I am a sinful man, O Lord," he said to Jesus (v. 8). Peter's response was similar to that of Isaiah's when he uttered, "Woe is me! For I am lost; for I am a man of unclean lips, and I dwell in the midst of a people of unclean lips; for my eyes have seen the King, the LORD of hosts!" (Isa. 6:5). Which shouldn't be surprising when we remember Peter and Isaiah said this while in the presence of the same person (John 12:41). As we already discussed, what's most intriguing about both of their reactions is that being in God's company didn't inspire praise first but confession. A depth of self-awareness accompanied with real-life fear. Both men understood themselves differently at the sight of God as, if by proximity, their hearts and their nature were laid bare and exposed to the light. His very being stood in moral contrast to theirs to the point that they had no inward justification to quench the truth about themselves. Being near the One who is light, and who has no darkness within Himself (1 John 1:5) illuminated their consciences to understand something very simple: that God was holy and they were not. Holiness makes honesty an obligation. Whether we see ourselves as a communicator of God's truth like Isaiah or a person with a collar colored blue, our titles tell us little about who we are *really*. Whatever we do and however we identify, when near God, we will see the truth and nothing but it. That what God is, we are not. Holy.

God is holy, so then, God is also sinless. To say that God is sinless is to say that God is without fault. Or to say that God is without fault is to say that God is morally pure. It might be difficult or at least interesting to imagine a being so different from us in that regard. One in whose mouth you'd be hard pressed to find deceit (1 Pet. 2:22) and whose eyes are too pure to look on anything wicked (Hab. 1:13), but even if it's difficult to imagine, we dare not imagine Him any other way. At the point when we begin to think of God as being anything other than holy is the moment we are imagining a completely different god altogether.

Moral Perfection and the Law

If we need some evidence proving the moral perfection of God, the law provides it. "As the holiness of the scripture demonstrates the divinity of its Author; so the holiness of the law doth the purity of the Lawgiver."[1] Our relationship to the law isn't worth celebrating fourteen days into February. However we learned about it, whether through counsel or conscience, we responded by resisting all of the goodness it had to offer, proving something deep and dark about ourselves. Mainly that we don't like to be like God. That's not to say that our sinfulness isn't a parody and a rather silly way of deifying ourselves. The serpent still incentivizes unbelief by promising that it will make us "like God," but our motive has never been to be like God in terms of righteousness but of rights. We lust after ultimate authority, plant our flag in shallow soil, and claim ourselves, and others, as our property. It's not until the law is put before us

---

[1] Stephen Charnock, *Discourses upon the Existence and Attributes of God*, volumes 1–2 (New York: Robert Carter & Brothers, 1874), 128.

that in its mirror, we see that we haven't become like God at all. We have only imaged Satan. This is because "the law is holy, and the commandment is holy and righteous and good" (Rom. 7:12). The law is holy because the Giver of it is, and responding to it in complete obedience (if possible) would've reckoned us all good. Problem is, "No one is good but God" (Mark 10:18)—as in, no one is holy but God.

The law tells us about the ethical nature of God if we look at it closely. Observing it like a curious child in its mother's lap, the first five precepts of the Decalogue (the Ten Commandments) reveal God's worth. The inverse of the first tenet—to have no other gods but God—would be an idolatrous endorsement if it were reversed and reshaped to command Israel to "have other gods before God." If on Mount Sinai, God thundered those words, the calf covered in gold, built right after the smoke cleared, would've been an affront to God that God Himself provoked. That is to say that God would be a recommender of wickedness. And what is wickedness anyway if not the refusal to honor God as God? Commanding anything other than absolute allegiance to Himself would not only be an evil for which God would require atonement for but also the promotion of a lie. The lie being that other gods, made by hands or thoughts or whatever, could in fact be God, too. As if they created the heavens and the earth; as if before anything made that was made, they existed. As if they could deliver on their promises or save or justify or sanctify a sinner. But only a devil would tell such stories.

And so it stands that God could never command us away from worshiping Himself. "Can he ever abrogate the command of love to himself without showing some contempt of his own excellence and very being? Before he can enjoin a creature not to love him, he must make himself unworthy of love and worthy of hatred; this would be the highest unrighteousness, to order us to hate that which is only worthy of our highest affections."[2]

If you squint your eyes a bit and place your hand on your chin while interrogating the second set of commands, in them you'll discover more of what God is like. What He commands of Israel there, is what He is in Himself. Love is not God, but God is love, and so being, He is active in how He gives it away. Murder, theft, adultery, dishonesty, and covetousness are a set of behaviors and heart postures that don't exist in God, not merely because He is love but because He is holy. Holiness is what makes real love possible. Without it, love is purely sentimental, easily misplaced, and unconditionally conditional. Being morally perfect positions God's love as a living thing that won't and literally

---

[2] Ibid., 130–31.

can't dishonor creation, so imagine again, the reversal of the duty to love our neighbor. "Thou shall murder, steal, commit adultery, lie, and covet" would, if commanded by God, reveal Him as a terror. A hater of all that He's made and One resolute on destroying and stripping all humans of their dignity. The half-hearted, self-centered, idol-prone love we model so well would be the ultimate ideal and the very definition of it, for there would be no moral standard beckoning us higher. God would be an instigator of hatred, and our obedience to such an animalistic way of life would make earth as we know it hell as its always been.

What, or should I say "who," I've described above sounds more like Satan than it does God, but who do you suppose we are imaging God as when His holiness is disregarded in our definitions of Him? God's being is antithetical to every way the world functions (1 John 2:16). Both transcendentally and ethically. Peter and Isaiah's experiences bear witness to this. In the same way, our natural repudiation of the law as it's taught, read, preached, and sung to us in an unconverted state reveals our sinfulness (Rom. 7:7). Our sinful nature is the very reason for a necessary "woe" in response to the presence of the Holy One. The law magnifies our darkness because its giver *is* light. It reveals our impurities because its giver *is* pure.

Moral Perfection and the Christ

In a real sense, the law helps us understand God. Behind its commands are fingerprints imprinted by a holy hand; but even then, the law paints a picture that's still insufficient. Like shaking the Polaroid only to find it incomplete. What then do we look to in order to explain more of what God is like? Or to be more specific, what does God's holiness look like in real life? I mean, we can ask to see His glory, but it's either death or a cleft available to us if God allows Himself to be seen. Thankfully, what Moses asked for in Exodus 33:18 ("Please show me your glory"), he stood in front of in Matthew 17:2–3 ("And he was transfigured before them, and his face shone like the sun, and his clothes became white as light. And behold, there appeared to them Moses and Elijah, talking with him"). He'd received those heavy, heavy stones and delivered them to Israel, for the law was given through him (John 1:17), but we should put a praise shout and a loud hallelujah right there, because after Moses came One who showed us *exactly* what God's holy, holy, holiness looked like.

Right after John told us about the Word (also known as Jesus on our side of the incarnation) being God and with God, he writes that no one has ever seen God but that Jesus has made Him known (John 1:18). I'm no Greek scholar but

I'll put my native tongue to the side for a second to draw attention to the word *eksēgéomai* which, translated, means that Jesus has *explained* God, or depending on which version of the Bible you read, "Jesus has *declared* Him." It's the root word of the theological term "exegesis." To draw this out even more, Jesus Christ, then, is "the exegesis of God, the exposition of his hidden reality."[3] If God were a sermon, Jesus would be the only one qualified to exposit it. He is the "image of the invisible God" and the "exact imprint of his nature" (Col. 1:15; Heb. 1:3); therefore, as Michael Reeves rightly put it, "Our definition of God must be built on the Son who reveals Him."[4]

What do we learn about God's moral perfection by looking at the Son, then? Well, we discover that as God is, the Son is also. He too is sinless, without blemish, morally pure, spotless, unconvictable, holy. On earth, He committed no sin nor was there any sin in Him (1 Pet. 2:22; 1 John 3:5).

Where our culture tends to be ignorant to the moral nature of God, demons aren't. Which is ironic that these fallen beings, relegated to darkness as they await an

---

[3] Bruce Milne, *The Message of John* (Downers Grove, IL: InterVarsity Press, 1993), 50.

[4] Michael Reeves, *Delighting in the Trinity* (Downers Grove, IL: InterVarsity Press, 2012), 22.

eternal heat, will testify that Jesus is the "Holy One of God" (Luke 4:34) much quicker than our kind might. They know what that means. As for us, we might say Jesus was a good man worth emulating, but what does "good" mean to us, really? To many, He is good insofar as He fits within the moral standards of society. Well-mannered, generous, fair, nonviolent, tolerant, vegan, polite, and inclusive. This Jesus is a good one, perhaps, but would He be a Holy One? That is the real question, and in response, I must say that holiness (and goodness) should never be determined by the whims, wishes, and standards of a created thing or even a whole culture. Especially when that culture's ideas are so easily influenced by the deceitful hearts within it, as well as its overall mutability, taking different shapes in conformity to its era. Jesus condescended with a dictionary in hand. It is Him, every bit of God, in the likeness of men, that translates the invisible. Disregarding the use of metaphor for a second, all I mean to say is this: God defines God.

I've paid a lot of attention to Jesus and how He navigated temptation in the wild (Luke 4:1–13). Being able to observe the ways and reasons Christ resisted the provocations of Satan creates for me another avenue to understand holiness. It's seeing what holiness does when tested that turns it to the side so different angles of the same image can be captured. After Jesus was washed in the river

Jordan, the Spirit that rested on Him like a dove led Him into the wilderness. There for forty days, belly empty, body less than strong, evidence of His full humanity and the rights He relinquished to be as weak as this, He's tempted to make bread. I know, I know—flour, yeast, eggs, milk, and baking powder don't exist in the wild, but Satan knew none of that mattered if Jesus was the Son of God. Since the beginning of time, Jesus has been creating and sustaining through supernatural means. As the divine Word in flesh, He could transform stones into loaves by the power of His speech (hence Satan telling Jesus to "command the stones") just as He did with light. Not only that, He could also access within Himself that creative agency displayed to Israel when from the sky came bread from heaven (manna). I can see it now, the devil pointing his finger at the stones scattered about the desert, hoping Jesus would remember His divine power and authority and leverage it to replace the nothing in His stomach. And I mean, He could if He *wanted* to—He is God, after all. But would He and did He *want* to? How would holiness involve itself?

Here He is, in the wilderness hungry as ever, the devil determined to use food as bait, hoping the Second Adam would be like the first. Not being one to entertain a demon for too long, Jesus pulls from Deuteronomy and quotes Moses' words in response to the tempter: "Man does not live by bread alone," the rest of the sentence being, "but man lives by every word that comes from the mouth of the LORD" (Deut. 8:3). This is holiness in action.

Notice that Jesus speaks no other words but God's own and that His complete refusal to participate in the devil's scheme comes out of His commitment to the Father He's always loved. Let's say, if possible, He just so happened to let the thought sit in His mind too long, saw the stones and tasted the bread. The line between temptation and sin would've vanished and the Son would've become a sinner an inch after His foot crossed it. Not primarily because of the chew either but because of what utilizing His divine power and the bite that benefited from it would've said about God. Dissect the words: "Man does not live by bread alone, but man lives by every word that comes from the mouth of God" (NKJV) and you'll see what I mean. The morally pure, spotless lamb that is Jesus knew that food— though a legitimate need—was not an ultimate need. His continuing on earth, alive and well in His body, was not solely dependent on food but on the God it comes from. To listen to the devil and command the stones would've been to distrust God's ability to sustain the Son. But also, a holy God cannot be a self-serving God. Even though at Jesus' command, a rock could become a meal, He would not utilize His powers to serve Himself. Sin at its core is selfish. Holiness at its core is self-giving. Water into wine, five loaves and two fish, these are instances when you'd see Jesus satiate a belly and a body as only He knew how. Employing His power to offer provision to others instead of Himself. Surely, the devil knew (or maybe he didn't) but didn't care that Jesus had come to serve and not be served and that His body would be given as a ransom for many. And because of that, Jesus didn't have to concern Himself with the loud noises coming from His stomach or the fear that one more day without food might kill Him. Of course He would die, one day. And it wouldn't be because He starved to death but because He laid His life down.

Every quote from Jesus came from the same book, Deuteronomy. When the devil suggested that Jesus bow down and worship him (what a silly, silly demon to even say such a thing), Jesus countered with, "You shall worship the Lord your God, and Him only shall you serve" (Luke 4:8 (ESV); c.f. Deut. 6:13). The exclusivity of worship, God alone being worthy of it, is shown as an aspect of holiness. It's a law Jesus was too holy, holy, holy to disobey. Along with the final demonic proposition to throw Himself down from the temple. Taking off from it, leaping into the wind, supposing the angels would indeed come to His rescue would've been the act of putting God to the test. The Son would've replicated the sin of Israel—doubting God and challenging Him to prove that He'll keep His promises (Deut. 6:16). But, of course, God will keep His promise to the Son, and the Son knows this because He *knows* God. Satan had claim on everybody who has lived. From Adam to Abraham. From Moses to David. From Solomon to Isaiah. From Malachi to me and you. Born of flesh and blood, nobody ever, has had the moral freedom and innate power to resist Satan so effectively except Jesus because truly, truly I say to you, Satan had no claim on Him (John 14:30)—only God did.

Now, what can we say about the moral perfection of God after observing the Son? That it's bright. We squint at it with our forearm beneath our brow bone, hoping the sight of it won't bury us. Did you see how different we are from Him? Even when enfleshed, those temptations from without found no place to land. Eve couldn't remain faithful beyond one question, yet the Son, thirty-three years after being born, remained holy the entire time.

I've tried to envision what it must be like to have a clean heart always. To see money and recognize it as being only paper and provision, not an idol or an identity. To see a woman and just see a woman. Or to see a woman and remember God. To be reviled and not have to deal with pride poking at you to say something back, begging you to prove that you're not as weak as you know you are; and when you do return the favor, sinning because of sin, the conscience reminds you of it. What sin did Jesus have to reminisce over? Adam's, I'm sure. And how everyone that came after him looked just like their father. Stephen Charnock said, "It is not a defect in God that he cannot do evil, but a fullness and excellency of power; as it is not a weakness in the light but the perfection of it, that it is unable to produce darkness."[5] Jesus, born into Adam's lineage but without his sinful nature, showed us what it really means to be morally perfect.

There was enough evidence to prove Jesus was guiltless, but the accusations of His having a different nature were commonplace still. Some said He partnered with Satan to cast out demons and that it was possible that the same demons He called out lived inside of Him too (Matt. 12:24). Others said that He was not from God; in other words, He was not from heaven but from the earth (John 9:16). Still others called Him not only demon-possessed, but a glutton and a drunkard for dining with sinners, and outright insane (Luke 7:34; John 10:20). These accusations amount to the assumption that His human nature was all there was to Him and nothing more. That His heart was without divine light, darkened by the bite in Adam's teeth

---

[5] Charnock, *Discourses upon the Existence and Attributes of God*, 125.

and the rebellion caught in his bones. That He too was only born of flesh and blood with no prior existence, just like the rest of us, a direct contradiction to His testimony of being alive before any flesh was born (John 8:52–58). That He was simply an ordinary man with a blasphemous mouth, a gluttonous stomach, and a drunken way of life. Another group of men fixed their mouths to say that they knew He was a sinner (John 9:24), but they actually didn't know what they were talking about or who they were talking to. Projecting their own sinfulness onto the Holy One was one form of resisting the truth. Evading accountability through accusation. If Jesus was as sinful as they claimed, everything He said about Himself would be a lie, justifying their unbelief. But if Jesus was as holy as He seemed, then everything He said about Himself, God, their heart, their world, and the world to come was true and worthy to be believed.

Moral Perfection and Our Unbelief

I suppose that for them and especially us, believing what God has said is parallel with who we believe God to be. What if in our unbelief, there exists some part of us that doesn't think too highly of the moral perfection of God? Is that not what the root of all sin is anyway? Not believing that God is honest to the point that we refuse to honor who He is because we don't believe what He's said? Take Eve, for example, who'd been told most likely by Adam, who'd been told by God, that the Tree of the Knowledge of Good and Evil shouldn't be consumed and that once it was, death would be immediate. I don't know how long she denied the tree's hand, refusing to delight in its perceived goodness, but however long it was, this obedience was owed to her faith in what God said about it. Her subjective thoughts and feelings about the tree didn't determine the tree's quality or if it was morally acceptable to partake of because God's Word is what relegated the tree as off-limits. Regardless of how it might've looked, how it might've tasted, or how real her affections for it were, it was as deadly as the devil who came into the garden with a question. To her, he asked, "Did God actually say, 'You shall not eat of any tree in the garden'?" To her, he lied, "You will not surely die" (Gen. 3:1, 4). Of course we all know what happened after this. We know that Eve took from the tree, ate the fruit, handed some to Adam, who had his share too. But do we know why? At the moment Eve believed the word of the serpent, rebelling against the word of God, her misplaced faith reflected what she believed about the holiness of God. To her, God—not the serpent—was the liar among them.

Not many people would dare call God a liar out loud, lest they be guilty of blasphemy and kept from forgiveness. What the mouth doesn't say, though, the heart still reveals. How we live is the evidence of what we believe about God. If Lord, we serve. If Creator, we're humble. If Savior, we trust. All of the above wasn't discerned without help. It was communicated through the world and the Word. The problem with our nature is that it corrupts our minds, inflates our ego, meddles with our vision, and darkens our understanding so that when God decides to tell us anything, we determine its integrity by how we feel over who God has revealed Himself to be. That is not to say that all unbelief is emotional, but it is to say that our decision-making in regards to what we believe about God is never isolated from our affections.[6]

Before we are unchained from sin, as slaves and lovers of it, truth is resisted because it demands something from us. It tells the heart what the heart refuses to acknowledge. That it is not as happy as the smile it manufactures or as full as it claims to be. It is a scary thing to hear the truth and actually believe it as that. If through the power of another's resurrection, we actually decide to finally agree

---

[6] Thomas Chalmers, *The Expulsive Power of a New Affection* (Wheaton, IL: Crossway, 2020).

with God, that He is the Creator of everything and therefore has claim on everything, including the heart, mind, and body, then we are obligated to give to God what He rightly deserves: our entire self. This is an impossible thing if in fact you believe what the devil has told you. That you are all the god you need. That every gift given to men, including everything from sex to the sun, is yours to exploit. To squeeze the beauty out of everything until it is no longer good but god. The inevitable consequence of not believing what God has said about Himself is to take what God has made and call it Lord. Among other things, not believing that God is telling the truth about sin and death must mean that there are no consequences, no hell, no judgment. If He is *just* love and not judge, which is no love at all really, then we can rebel without accountability. This is the pseudo-freedom that sinners prefer. Life on their terms. Heaven and hell at the same time. If we are brave enough to actually believe that God is who He says He is, we are left with one choice: worship. But if we want to be the center of attention, the source of our joy, and the final authority of our lives, then, in our minds, God cannot be holy; He must be just like us. A sinner.

It is good news that the maintenance of God's righteousness is independent of our faith in it. Whether we believe He is holy or not, He will always be what He's always been. God's eternal sinlessness means many things, but in the simplest terms, to us, God cannot lie. He is "not man, that he should lie" and He is the God who "never lies" (Num. 23:19; Titus 1:2). As holy, God sees things as they are. The ultimate realist who will never distort the truth or be ignorant of it. The one who provided Eve with an alternate reality said, "You will not surely die" (Gen. 3:4). The words might've sounded sincere, as in, true. Authentic. Liars are like that though—good ones, that is. Able to lie without breaking their smile. Being at ease with deception is suitable for Satan because according to Jesus, he is the "father of lies" who "doesn't stand in the truth" and when lying, he speaks "out of his own character" (John 8:44). There is a world of difference between Satan and God, you see, but in our struggle to believe God, it's as if we sometimes suspect that God assumes a different, darker nature. That when Paul says that nothing can "separate us from the love of God" (Rom. 8:39), we refuse the notion as being real toward anybody and especially us. How many of our sins began with the belief that God didn't love us truly? Who is it, then, whom we believed on those days? Not God.

One way Jesus addressed Israel's unbelief is by engaging them with a question on His moral purity. He said, "Which of you convicts me of sin? If I tell you the truth, why do you not believe me?" (John 8:46). If this same question were asked by anybody other than God, they would be a narcissist, blind, or both. The disciple whom Jesus loved wrote, "If we say we have no sin, we deceive ourselves, and the truth is not in us" (1 John 1:8). Any human who stands next to God's law, lifts up their haughty head, and tells the world that they have been just as good as it requires is lying. Only Jesus can stand next to the law and it be a spitting image. Only Jesus can say what He said about Himself and it be true. Such as how He *always* does what is pleasing to God (John 8:29). Always. As in, at all times, consistently, perpetually, night and day, the Son pleases the Father. This testimony was confirmed by the Father who spoke over the Son during His baptism with the ultimate affirmation, "This is my beloved Son, with whom I am well pleased" (Matt. 3:17). Without the Father's witness and the Son's sinless life, every claim made by Jesus would certainly be delusions of grandeur and worse, Jesus would hold rank among the false prophets of old. About this, C. S. Lewis said, "A man who was merely a man and said the sort of things Jesus said would not be a great moral teacher. He would either be a lunatic—on the level with the man who says he is a poached egg—or else he would be the Devil of Hell."[7]

---

[7] C. S. Lewis, *Mere Christianity* (New York: HarperCollins, 1952), 55–56.

It seems like a reach to say it as C. S. did, that Jesus is either God (and thus holy, not a liar) or that Jesus is a lunatic. But how else could you describe Him if He were lying about being the resurrection and the life? About His claim that He and the Father are one? About His statement that before Abraham was, He was too, claiming eternality? About His declaration that He has authority to forgive sins and that if someone decides not to believe Him, they will die in their sins? There is no gray area when it comes to how evil it would be if Jesus were lying about these things. Offering Himself up as bread to the hungry and water to the thirsty only to turn around and be neither food nor drink but a liar in need of both. If this were the case, we would be wise in our denial of Him. No one with good sense should give their allegiance to a lie. However, that is not the option we are given because He is neither lunatic nor false prophet; He is the way, *the truth*, and the life. As C. S. Lewis added, "You can shut him up for a fool, you can spit at him and kill him as a demon or you can fall at his feet and call him Lord and God."[8]

If there is anything I want you to take to heart, it's this: because God is holy, all that He says is true and all that He does is good. In John's gospel alone, Jesus says

---

[8] Ibid.

"I tell you the truth" upwards of twenty-five times.[9] Jesus was being repetitive to prove a point: that all He has said is true because He in fact is a truthful person. To say "*I tell you the truth*" means Jesus is assuring us not only of the importance of whatever statement He makes; He is equally assuring us of His true and holy character behind those statements. The message is trustworthy and right, He wants us to know, and so is the mouth that declares it. Or consider Jeremiah 2:5 where God says, "What wrong did your fathers find in me that they went far from me, and went after worthlessness, and became worthless?" Having an erroneous view of the unblemished ethical nature of God tempts us to doubt His word, leading to the denial of His worth. If His character isn't trusted, His words won't be believed.

One thing about life, and the people we come to know as we go about it, is that it's ripe with sin and suffering. There is not a day that goes by that we are not sinned against in some way. Everybody ain't loved everybody well. We were born into a world where cheeks aren't easily

---

[9] This amount of frequency with which this phrase appears depends on which translation is used. In the New Living Translation, this phrase is found twenty-five times in the book of John. When phrased differently in other translations, the point is still clear in all the relevant passages: Jesus is trying to help us see He is telling us the truth.

turned but shoulders cold as a bad dream are handed out liberally. Some of us still grieve the memories we wish we had, with our fathers in them instead of without them. Among us are those who have been on the other end of traumas so ungodly, the body forgot the pain to protect itself from the shock of remembering. I can't imagine how many hands we'd need to number the times we've been lied to, talked about, objectified, ignored, abandoned, rejected, and abused. If you think about it, some of the sins we own are those we acquired as a way to cope. Withholding love because it's been taken advantage of. Easily given to rage or irritation because in us is a hurt we're too afraid to name. This world has never been as safe as heaven, so for protection, we exist in it guarding ourselves from the trauma of it. And I wonder if underneath our doubt, way at the bottom of it, is a suspicion that God isn't safe either. That He is just like the father that left us, the mother that forgot to nurture us, the friend that didn't listen to us, and the folks in positions of power that abused us. So when God reveals Himself as our heavenly parent, a faithful friend, and our Lord, we don't relinquish control, surrendering our wills because we've mistakenly projected onto God the nature of those who have sinned against us. Seeing heaven through the lens of earth. Eyeing God through the lens of fear.

Hear this: God's words and works can be trusted because it is impossible for God to sin against you. If He could, He wouldn't be God. There is an untainted goodness in Jesus, the spotless Savior, the unblemished Lamb. To believe otherwise is to imagine an entirely different being. "He can no more act contrary to this goodness in any of his actions than he can un-god Himself."[10] Since He is God, a Holy One at that, in all of His dealings with us, He is always good. Always. As in, at all times, consistently, perpetually, night and day. "The Rock, his work is perfect, for all his ways are justice. A God of faithfulness and without iniquity, just and upright is he" (Deut. 32:4). Consider the law again, and how it reveals God's nature. What God has commanded, He Himself embodies. God honors (Exod. 20:3–12). God is life-giving (v. 13). God is covenant-keeping (v. 14). God takes what is His and gives it away (v. 15). God tells the truth (v. 16). God is content, never needy for anything. Only jealous for our whole heart, to have and to hold (v. 17). God's perfection is in fact what we want most in our neighbors. We desire a measure of integrity and neighborly love that we've sometimes seen in the holiest of

---

[10] Charnock, *Discourses upon the Existence and Attributes of God*, 224.

saints, but behold the Holy One. In His perfection, all He will ever be is good to us, good *for* us.

Even when suffering breaks in, tempting us to "curse God and die" (Job. 2:9), remember the God in whom your suffering was given an allowance. Of Him it is said, "though he cause grief, he will have compassion according to the abundance of his steadfast love" (Lam. 3:32). Even when it hurts, it's as not as though God has somehow changed, becoming cruel or inflicting pain without purpose. It's not as if when everything collapses in on itself, God will leave you to pick up the pieces. As the Holy God, He is present in our pain with the steady promise of redeeming it for our good. "And we know that for those who love God all things work together for good, for those who are called according to his purpose" (Rom. 8:28). His transcendence makes this promise possible. If He was a derivative of the world, every uneasy circumstance would come without a leash. Independent of it, God is sovereign over it.

Now, this wouldn't be anything to lift a praise for if the Sovereign One was void of compassion. Of love. Of native holiness. What would it do for us to know He has power but not the impulse to use it for good? But our God is no politician, having authority without righteousness. Upon leaving heaven, He took part in all kinds of suffering that we may never fully grasp. The final blow was felt when the

Father poured out the cup of wrath on His sinless Son, for our sake. This is to say that Jesus is neither ignorant of suffering nor powerless because of it, but rather He knows it well. Well enough to offer empathy, yes, but also victorious enough to give us hope. As 1 Peter 5:10–11 would put it, "And after you have suffered a little while, the God of all grace, who has called you to his eternal glory in Christ, will himself restore, confirm, strengthen, and establish you. To him be the dominion forever and ever. Amen."

When there is a storm, believe God. When there is stillness, believe God. He is too holy to deceive. Too holy to lead you anywhere but to truth. When God tells you to "cast your cares on him because he cares for you," He is not lying (1 Pet. 5:7). There was no deceit found in His mouth then; search for it now and you will only find light. He can be trusted with our cares because a holy God cannot be an apathetic God.

How can I say that? Let us look to Jesus another time, again, on a boat. When the waters threatened to swallow their boat whole, the disciples questioned the compassion of the sleeping Savior by saying, "Teacher, do you not care that we are perishing?" (Mark 4:38). It's comical how unbelief works. How it made them think Jesus was unconcerned about their lives when He'd come to earth to save it in the first place. Just like them, we are in water-torn boats. On

59

land, we are the stranger bleeding on the roadside. Our only hope is for someone gentle and lowly to calm the storm and heal our wounds and carry our yoke. See the cross and believe the Lord upon it. He is greater than the great Samaritan. He cares to the point of death, so take Him at His word, giving Him your burdens, trading it for His peace.

When God tells you that your life will be lost if and when you try to save it, but losing it for His sake is where you will find it, believe Him. Christ will not allow you to find life any other way because there is no other way. Devils will tell you that it's possible to live without God, but reality as Christ told us is that there is no life outside of Him. After the crowd left Him to find life where there is none, Jesus asked the disciples if they wanted to leave too. Peter said, "Lord, to whom shall we go? You have the words of eternal life, and we have believed, and have come to know, that you are the Holy One of God" (John 6:68–69). Peter figured out that the Holy One can't lie to them. That His words are true and should be believed. That where God is, life is too.

When God says that if you ask, it will be given to you, that if you seek, and you will find (Luke 11:9), believe Him. The act of asking feels trivial at the point that you believe in a God who will not answer when asked, as if He sees the knocking and ignores the person lifting the hand. God is not like us in this way, seeing the needs of others and scrolling to the next post, declining the call, denying relief. God is not an idol, a being that can't speak when spoken to, hear when prayed to, act when asked. On Mount Carmel, the difference between God and idols came down to the manifestation of one being lifeless, and therefore unable to answer prayers. To Baal they said, "O Baal, answer us!" The result? "But there was no voice, and no one answered" (1 Kings 18:26). The Holy God has life in Himself, forever aware of what we need before we even ask. You hear because He can. You speak because He always has. Your image is His, remember? The ability to communicate began with your being made by and for Him. Remove the lie from your mind that God does not listen, or speak, or act when asked. He is alive at all times. Answering every prayer. Sometimes a "yes." Other times a "no." Many times a "wait." And all three are answers. All three are governed by transcendent wisdom, for our good, always.

And what else should we expect from the Holy One? The Holy God who is good, all the time. All the time, the Holy God is good. This God is worthy to be believed.

Chapter 3

Holy, Holy Holy: Transcendence

MOSES NEVER SAW ANYTHING like it. He went into the wilderness expecting nothing new. Just bushes scattered about as usual. This time, one of the bushes he wouldn't usually pay any mind to was burning. Any other day, if a bush caught fire, it would burn. The smell of smoke atop its own ash is all that would be left. The one burning now was different, strange in every way. It burned and stayed the same shape. If there was any smoke at all, it wasn't from the branches but from the flame itself seeing that the fire was independent of the bush it danced inside of. The sight caught and kept Moses' attention, a bush burning but not consumed. Looking at it, he wondered why.

Then, the answer spoke.

God called to him out of the bush, "Moses, Moses!" And he said, "Here I am." Then [God] said, "Do not come near; take your sandals off

your feet, for the place on which you are stand-
ing is holy ground." And he said, "I am the God
of your father, the God of Abraham, the God
of Isaac, and the God of Jacob." And Moses
hid his face, for he was afraid to look at God.
(Exod. 3:4–6)

The reason the bush burned without being consumed
here in Exodus 3 is because of who was present in it. It was
the self-revelation of the transcendent God. Transcendence,
as we've dabbled in a bit earlier, is the "otherness" of God.
He is infinitely different. Ontologically set apart. Unique.
He transcends all categories unless the category has above
it the name of God and beside it in contrast is everything
else. Everything, meaning everything that exists. It's not
as though God is simply a better, more improved version
of humans. It's not that He is transcendent because He
simply knows more than us. No. When speaking of God's
transcendent knowledge, for example, it isn't simply that
He knows more, but that He knows everything—and to
know everything, He must be a being that exists in a way
that no creature can or ever will.

Isaiah asked the question, rhetorical of course, "Who
has directed the Spirit of the Lord, or who gave him counsel? Who did he consult? Who gave him understanding

and taught him the paths of justice? Who taught him knowledge and showed him the way of understanding?" (Isa. 40:14 csb). Think about that. And whatever it is that you thought about, whether it was the formation of a set of questions or the remembrance of what you already know about God as omniscient, recall when it was that you learned it. This knowledge of God, or anything really, wasn't innate. The only thing you knew when you were born was nothing. Through your parents' guidance, your teachers' teaching, your eyes watching, your studious studying, etc., you were able to do what all humans *have* to do: learn. With God, however, He never needed instruction at any point in time or before it. If He did, from where would He have gotten it?

Before this book—the paper, the hands that wrote it, the mother who birthed its author, the mothers before her who washed babies, greens, cotton fields, and West African floorboards—way, way before them, was earth, a garden, many trees, one forbidden, two people, one made first, the other second, both imaging one God in three persons who was here, before everything. Before everything, then, when the triune God existed with Himself, who would've given Him advice on how to make light? From what source other than Himself would He have sat down before, in a chair, pen and pad in hand, to take notes about how to make a universe? Darwin? Socrates? Plato? Aristotle? Einstein? Hawking? Google? Twitter? You?

God is altogether separate and not set apart to the degree that He is unreachable or unknowable but separate from us in that He exists differently than us. As the holy God, He is one of a kind. His uniqueness is what defines Him as holy for, as we've seen before, the word itself means "to cut" or "to separate." He is above us in His very *being*, totally different than us in how He exists.

Definitions of God's holiness have often been wrapped around the moral perfection of God, something we explored in the last chapter, which as we've seen, isn't excluded from the meaning but also not exclusive of it either. When it comes to our definition of God's holiness, we'd be right to include God's righteousness, but alongside that is God's "otherness." R. C. Sproul said this: "When the Bible calls God holy, it means primarily that God is transcendentally separate. He is so far above and beyond us that He seems almost totally foreign to us. To be holy is to be 'other,' to be different in a special way."[1] It seems to me that high-lighting the ethical implications of what *holy* means and not giving due diligence to the transcendental nature of the

---

[1] R. C. Sproul, *The Holiness of God* (Carol Stream, IL: Tyndale, 1985), 48.

term, theologians have made room for our understanding of holiness to be too narrow, eliminating a measure of awe and potentially additional reasons to be faithful.

Returning to the bush that wouldn't burn, how is God's transcendence observable? Because of the fact the plant was able to remain intact. What Moses saw was a bush— within it, a flame. The fire didn't reach for the stems or grab hold of the leaves; *it burned without any help*. The bush contained the flame, but the flame wasn't dependent on the bush. Concerning a bush ignited by anything other than God, the fire would *need* the bush, as its fuel, for its life. Each flame would derive every ounce of energy it required from what it burned. Once fire catches onto anything, whether it's a paper's edge or a forest's trees, it exists only because the thing does and the fire will only last as long as the thing it burns exists. Once the thing is consumed, the fire is gone, revealing how needy the flames were in the first place. But this bush burned without being consumed because the God who manifested Himself in it didn't need the leaves, the stems, or the branches for its fuel. All He needs is Himself. So it is with the flame. It wasn't dependent on the bush because it was totally independent of the bush.

What are we to discern from this theophany (a preincarnate, visible manifestation of God)? What does it reveal? That God is the epitome of independence. He is free in the truest sense of the word. Meaning, He is free from the need of anything else but Himself for Him to *be*. This is one fundamental difference between everything and God; because what is there to name that isn't dependent on something or someone for its life? Dependence is creaturely. Everything that *is* needs something outside of itself to both begin and continue. The very fact we all have a beginning distinguishes us from the I Am, who has life in Himself. The question is asked, "Who created God?" The answer is that God was not and cannot be created; He is because He is. Before the beginning, He was. After the end, He will be.

In the first sentence, on the first page, in the first book of God's Word, it reads: "In the beginning, God created the heavens and the earth" (Gen. 1:1). The beginning came out of someplace. Someone who had to be before anything else could. What this says about God is that He is self-existing. Alive, not from borrowed breath, but sustained by the life He has in Himself. God is not a derivative of anything since everything derived from Him. He is only able to give what He Himself is, which means when the world and time and the stars and the sun—and the first man to see it shine next to the first woman to make him laugh—were brought forth, their life came from His own. Having life and creative power from within to make and maintain everything that exists, compare God to us and see how different the two are. Let us create anything, and we need assistance. A writer needs a paper or a MacBook, not to mention a mind with memories given and ordained by someone other than chance. God only needs Himself. As God He is not dependent on His creation to do anything. He is distinct from it, and therefore He can never be controlled, challenged, or intimidated by it. If every sea in the world twisted itself into a hurricane, tall enough to meet the clouds, wide enough to cover a thousand cities, its knees would still bow and eventually break at God's command to "Be still." More than that, the seas couldn't twist into nothing anyway without His decree or permission, as if they had some ability to conspire against God or some inner life of their own apart from His word that holds them together. They cannot move one inch without Him saying so or without His knowledge, under His watchful eye and divine sovereignty. What can the world do to the God who formed it?

Being self-existing and independent has even more implications to which I don't have the time to put forward here, but another one worthy of our attention is how as self-existent and independent, God has no needs. "The God who made the world and everything in it, being Lord of heaven and earth, does not live in temples made by man, nor is he served by human hands, as though he needed anything, since he himself gives to all mankind life and breath and everything" (Acts 17:24–25). God's self-sufficiency means there is nothing lacking in God. He is immutably whole. Tozer said, "To admit the existence of a need in God is to admit incompleteness in the divine Being. Need is a creature-word and cannot be spoken of the Creator. God has a voluntary relation to everything He has made, but He has no necessary relation to anything outside of Himself. His interest in His creatures arises from His sovereign good pleasure, not from any need those creatures can supply nor from any completeness they can bring to Him who is complete in Himself."[2] If the rocks replaced the praise of millions who opted to withhold their love or keep quiet their worship, it would not leave God empty, as if He needed our praise to be complete. If and when we imagine a God who needs us for anything, we are dreaming of an idol and not the "I AM WHO I AM" (Exod. 3:14).

There's Nobody Like the Lord

For centuries Christians have known that God is God, incomparable to anything other than Himself. We put it in

---

[2] A. W. Tozer, *The Knowledge of the Holy* (New York: HarperCollins, 1978), 32.

our creeds, sing about it in our songs. The saints before us agreed with reality when saying, "Ain't nobody like Jesus" or "There's nobody like You, Lord." Both confessions came out of a faithful comparison, made with memories and observations that were put next to the Scriptures. They placed God beside anything and everything to see the difference between the two resulting in a right-now praise sent toward the Holy One. These aren't the musings of a theological romantic. It is the shared testimony of the psalmists and the prophets who wrote songs about and sent praises up for God's transcendence long before we did.

To say it again, "Ain't nobody like Jesus." And Scripture agrees. There are times when God, in showing the utter futility of idolatry, says to Israel, "To whom then will you liken God, or what likeness compare with him?" (Isa. 40:18) and "'To whom will you compare me, or who is my equal?' asks the Holy One" (Isa. 40:25 CSB). In prayers for deliverance, the psalmists often appeal to the uniqueness of God—His transcendence—as *reason to trust* that He will come to their aid: "Your righteousness, O God, reaches the high heavens. You who have done great things, O God, *who is like you?*" (Ps. 71:19, emphasis added). And "There is *none like you* among the gods, O Lord, nor are there any works like yours" (Ps. 86:8, emphasis added). When was the last time God's transcendence or holiness was your whole reason, your every motivation, to trust Him?

We don't only see transcendence on the mouths of worshipers or on the front end of prayers to God for help. After God does deliver, such as in the case of God's deliverance of Israel from Egypt, after-the-fact praise is given to the distinctiveness of God again, seeing that there is nobody and no one who can do the things God can do, like cause an entire community of people to walk through a sea on dry land. It seems fitting then to worship God by saying "Who among the gods is like You, O Lord? Who is like You—majestic in holiness, revered with praises, performing wonders?" (Exod. 15:11 Berean Study Bible).

The psalmists and the prophets were not being sentimental in their insistence that God is altogether different; they were being doctrinal. If they didn't know anything, at the very least they knew that in the beginning God created the heavens and the earth, and that very fact alone set God apart as a Being that is above and beyond the heavens and the earth that He'd created, including everything within it.

As incomparable as God is, it seems to me that one problem with us humans is that we become so used to the idea of God that we treat Him as commonplace. I think that may be our default, however. Treating God like He's ordinary might be a natural response when we're ignorant to who God has revealed Himself to be. Even with Moses, if he wasn't told not to come near, he would have. He had to be instructed on how to approach God, to not come too close, to remove his shoes and respect the sanctified ground underfoot. The same with Israel, who was warned not to touch the mountain God descended on, lest they be put to death following the irreverent approach. Devoid of awe, we reach behind the veil too quick to even notice the disrespect. We enter the Holies of Holies and treat the mercy seat like a footstool. The Lord's prayer begins in such a way that if one decided to let it sit on the mind for a bit, one might choose not to say anything at all. "Our Father in heaven, hallowed [holy] be your name." Around Him, the seraphim refuse to look. Before Him, Isaiah confessed. Seeing Him, Isaiah fell on his face. In front of Him, John fell at His feet like a body does once the soul leaves.

The Holy God is no regular being. He is so transcendent that Ezekiel was bereft of words when trying to explain his vision of God. Listen to his desperate attempt at description in Ezekiel 1:26–29 (emphasis added):

> And above the expanse over their heads there was the *likeness of* a throne, in appearance *like* sapphire; and seated above the *likeness of* a throne was a *likeness* with a human appearance.

And upward from what had the *appearance of* his waist I saw as it were gleaming metal, *like the appearance of* fire enclosed all around. And downward from what had the *appearance of* his waist I saw as it were the *appearance of* fire, and there was brightness around him. *Like the appearance of* the bow that is in the cloud on the day of rain, so was the appearance of the brightness all around. Such was the *appearance of* the *likeness of* the glory of the LORD. And when I saw it, I fell on my face.

Of all the words at his disposal, he couldn't find one accurate enough for what he saw. All he could think to do is make similes, depending on the term *likeness* as a sufficient replacement for what he couldn't be exact about. What other being do you know who transcends language? Who can't be pinned down by specificity at times?

Not considering transcendence in our idea of God leads to another error in our conception of Him. Since God is unique and in a class all by Himself, there are times when in an effort to either understand Him or explain Him, we take the attribute of God that resembles us most and make our human experience the lens by which we see God. Let's use the attribute "love," for example. We love the love of

God, as we should. For without it, we'd all be caged in between our heavy-handed flesh and the eternal damnation that awaits us as a consequence. We are prone to love the divine attributes that are most relatable to our own humanity or culture; this is possibly why God's love is esteemed more than His holiness in our day and time. We get love. Righteousness? Not so much. David Wells said this: "We assume we know what God's love is because it connects with our experience in a way that many of his other attributes do not. And why is this? The answer, obviously, is that there is no parallel in our experience to many of God's other attributes such as his eternality, omnipresence, omniscience, or omnipotence. But there is to his love."[3]

Love is a commonality we all share. Introduced to it at first by the people who wiped our behinds, bent their backs to ensure we stood up straight, clothed and kept our bellies full until we were old enough to fix our own plate. From there, we gathered and spread about the country acting out the love we inherited on friends and folks we made more than friends. Anxiously waiting for the day when our lovers used words to tell us that they love us back. Oh, we know what it's like to love and be loved, but what happens when

---

[3] David Wells, *God in the Whirlwind* (Wheaton, IL: Crossway, 2014), 79.

our lovely experiences become the primary framework by which we understand God? What happens is this: When we read the sentence, "God is love" disconnected from a fundamental understanding that God is "Holy, Holy, Holy," we interpret the text with our experiences as the commentary. Using our life as a cross reference, exegeting God with our world, we inevitably end up with a god made in our own image and then expect Him to behave just like us.

As finite beings, it's hard to trust in anything that doesn't accommodate us in some way; as an attribute of God, holiness feels too far from our reach. Love feels safe, tangible, good. We've touched love with our hands, snaked it between each finger like a wedding ring in search of a home. It makes sense why we'd want God to be the best of whatever love we've known then and in one sense, He is. But as transcendent and therefore unique, different, distinct, incomparable, and independent of the earth—the people, feelings, and events that defined love for us are an inadequate mirror to find God in. Our parents, friends, and lovers gave us whatever degree of love they were capable of gifting, and when opened, we all learned through some jaded maturity or disappointment how inconsistent it was. Their best was never good enough, no matter how sincere it was, because all of their love was tainted and twisted around a hard heart and their creaturely nature made it an insufficient substitute for God's.

Imagine how foolish we are, to grow up in a world of partially developed love, shaped by Adam's blood and generational trauma, only to look to that as the way God should be? No wonder our souls are so gray, fruit so scarce. In our attempt to make sense of God through our human lenses, we've actually lowered the bar for who God is. Becoming frustrated in His inability to be weak, we want God to be just like us because maybe then, faith wouldn't be such a task. But He can't and He won't because He is too holy to be like anyone other than Himself.

The Transcendent God

God is altogether different than any being you have ever known or will ever know. Not to be compared with any. His ways are not our ways, nor are His thoughts our thoughts. Literally. "For as the heavens are higher than the earth, so are my ways higher than your ways and my thoughts than your thoughts," says the Holy One in Isaiah 55:9. You look at the dirt and see a home for your plants; He looked at it and knew He'd name it Adam. Last night before the sun responded to God's command to "rise," the unlit part of the world rested while God neither slept nor slumbered. Sleep is an unnecessary task for God. His power comes from within Himself, endless, never suffering from lack. That's why we can reach out and ask Him and trust Him and beg Him for ability, for power or peace, even in the dead of night. He's the only one who has it to give.

The wisdom and otherness displayed in His gospel is other-worldly as well. Through wisdom, what God set in motion as the criteria for forgiveness is truly unbelievable. With Allah, along with the god of Joseph Smith (Mormonism) and Charles Taze Russell (Jehovah's Witnesses), just to name a few, heaven can only be reached by way of works. Which, in consideration of the human mind, it makes sense that a god created in our image would require its servants to work, and strive, and toil, to earn the forgiveness that eludes us all. Grace isn't something we understand or extend fundamentally. It's a foreign concept that's come to us by way of Jesus. He being the embodiment of heaven coming to earth so that the guilty can be declared innocent on the basis of grace and grace alone. Even in this, the transcendent God is unveiled for us. The glory cloud is brought low enough for us to peek behind the smoke. Every false religion and the god it represents reveals itself as a religion born from the earth in the way it offers up salvation only to those that deserve it. But the God who cannot be compared, who has all wisdom, in using what the world perceives as foolish, did the unthinkable. He made it so that the only object the undeserving have to offer in exchange for pardon is faith. Arranging salvation this way is incomprehensible, yes, indeed it is holy. Set apart. Different from the way any other god would set up the way of redemption. "Who is a God like You, who pardons iniquity and passes over the transgression of the remnant of His inheritance—who does not retain His anger forever, because He delights in loving devotion?" (Mic. 7:18 Berean Study Bible). No one is, Micah. No one.

Another reason God differs from everything creaturely is because He is changeless or "immutable," as theologians would say. About Himself, He said, "For I the LORD do not change . . ." (Mal. 3:6). Everything around us is mutable. Everything is in a constant state of becoming. As time progresses (changes), we adjust, develop, shift, transform. Both for good and bad. We may not like how mutability affects our waistline or the glow in our face, but it is a gift that we are given to change, for without it, sanctification itself would be impossible. If allowed to speak more than it should, unbelief may tell you all kinds of things about the changeless nature of God. Don't let life get hard; you may be tempted to believe that God has changed because your circumstances have, but if that were the case, He wouldn't be God, He'd be you. That's the way of the double-minded man. Trusting God on Tuesday morning, doubting God by evening. Supposing that what made Him trustworthy is no longer found perfect in Him now as if He is only good sometimes. God's perfections don't grow nor wain. With Him, "there is no variation or shadow due to change" (James 1:17). There is no greater stability in all of the created universe except in God.

I must say it again, "There is no one like You, Lord." No one is Creator but God. No one has all power but God. No one knows the beginning and the end all at the same time except God. No one is all-wise but God. No one can forgive sins but God. No one can grant eternal life but God. No one has no one to answer to but God. No one is unchanging but God. No one is good but God. Who then can we compare Him to except Himself? It's only when we become *like Him* that we can then be considered to be different than the world in which we live, but God need not come near to anyone to be made unique, He already *is*.

Chapter 4

Unholy gods: Idolatry

What comes into our minds when we think about God is the most important thing about us.

A. W. TOZER CAME up with that, not me.[1] But I wanted his sentence to begin this chapter because it's revelatory, especially when put as a question. If Mr. Tozer were to have asked, "What comes into your mind when you think about God?", the answer, if not restrained by self-deception, would tell you a lot about yourself. And potentially, how much of yourself is in love with a lie.

What we think about God and what we believe about God don't always resemble, although we'd like them to. We want to look in the mirror and see the same face, but the fallenness of everything means that there are invisible

---

[1] A. W. Tozer, *The Knowledge of the Holy* (New York: HarperCollins, 1961), 1.

contradictions everywhere. We will *say* that God is holy, as this book is designed to show, but there are little gods we may or may not have given a name to that have earned that attribution by our misplaced faith in them. I say this because when you interrogate the *why* behind our various forms of idol worship, the language used describes a holy thing, and the expectation of the worshiper sounds like faith.

An Old Testament illustration of this happened at the bottom of a mountain. God's people, deluded by impatience, irked that Moses was still at the top of it with Yahweh, asked Aaron to make them gods. The first evidence that their hope was an unholy one was made plain by their own words: *make* and *gods*. The two words should've gotten caught in their throat followed by a cough, a sneeze, a hiccup, some bodily reaction to show how ridiculous they were being. By definition, a real god can't *be made*; a real god *makes*, and in so doing, his aseity is proven. That's a fancy word summarizing how God is self-existing. He is uncreated and therefore sustained by no one except Himself. As we've already discussed, His life is His, not borrowed or given through some other means. He is as unlimited as the sky is wide. The same blue one He made without heaven's help. The universe is His doing alone. His hands are His to hold for strength, if He ever needed it, but He won't because a real God has no needs (Acts 17:25).

Ironically, I've projected a mirage of this same need-lessness on others at times, which is *still* me functioning out of my inherent neediness. The want of self-preservation and/or protection. God concerns Himself with neither. He can't exist in any other way than how He's always been, the self-sufficient One. So then, when He does decide to make something, He does it not to fill a void but to give opportunity for all that He is to be known by another.[2] Existing completely independent and categorically different from all that He's made (holy transcendence, as we've seen) allows God to operate freely with His creation. He is able to save, deliver, listen, respond, comfort, restrain, transform, create, destroy, whenever and however He decides. Unlike a calf *made* . . . of gold.

The children, sons and daughters, wives, and so on, unclasped the shiny gold things from their ears. Slid the rings off of their fingers, eyeing each as it was handed over to Aaron, anticipating what god he'd make from the same Egyptian metal they'd worn to pretty themselves. They'd decided that jewelry, when melted and molded into a cow,

---

[2] For more on this concept, see *Delighting in the Trinity* by Michael Reeves, particularly chapter 2, which is titled "Creation: The Father's Love Overflows" (Downers Grove, IL: 2012), 39–62.

could be for them what Yahweh had already demonstrated. They wanted a god that would "go before them" despite the newborn memory of the cloud by day and the fire by night. Their God had stood between them, Egypt and Israel, as protection from Pharaoh's heavy hand (Exod. 14:19–20). When the sun was up, God went before them in a pillar of cloud, guiding every foot to its intentional place. Night time could come just as quickly as the morning, moving the sun below the earth, but there to mitigate the darkness, a pillar of fire (Exod. 13:21–22). Useful for warmth, a comfort. And light, a leader. If they wanted guidance and protection—a necessary desire; sinless, in fact—they knew exactly who to trust in order to receive it. But as the psalmist described, "They exchanged the glory of God for the image of an ox that eats grass. They forgot God, their Savior, who had done great things in Egypt" (Ps. 106:20–21).

Idolatry always involves an exchange. It is a magician's act in which the holy is traded for the profane. The unique for the common. The transcendent for the earthly. The Creator for the creature. Exchanging the truth about God for a lie, as Paul puts it, leads to creaturely worship, glorying in a made thing (Rom. 1:25). And as I've said in another way, made things treated as a god or idols aren't holy in and of themselves. They all lack that transcendental value and moral purity that God possesses in Himself.

Which is interesting to think about really. How in our quest for an invented god, we're always compelled to worship someone or something that exists just like we do with the futile expectation that they'll succeed in being able to give us what is beyond their reach.

Israel's wish was for the golden calf to take the lead on getting them to where the milk and honey was, protecting them on the way. But remember, the golden calf wasn't a real god, and because of its makeup, it wasn't transcendent like the real One either. During the day, God had the ability to present Himself as a cloud. At night, a fire. No creature can get beyond itself or the body it lives in, but God is not like us; He is not restricted by anything, in heaven or on earth, when it comes to how He chooses to show up. The golden calf would forever remain as it was, unless given over to the heat, never having the power to reveal itself differently so as to be flexible in its leadership of Israel: unholy.

Idols are also local. Restrained by space and time, their fellow creature. How did Israel expect a golden calf to guide them if it couldn't move on its own? It could only go as far as a few humans were willing to take it. Them going *with* it, instead of it going *before* them. As it went, with their help, it also couldn't foresee what was ahead of them, not simply in terms of direction, but also time. Their true help would eventually say through Isaiah, "I am God, and there is none like me, declaring the end from the beginning and from ancient times things not yet done . . ." (Isa. 46:9–10).

Again, being set apart in every way possible, their real God, utterly unique, existed outside of time. Time, like them and their precious calf, was a creature. God's relationship to time is that of a sovereign, not a servant. So whatever time called a memory, God saw presently. Along with it were those soon to come, the marrow of the prophetic, almost-but-not-yet-here events that people wish upon a star to find out about. He sees it all, from the beginning to the end. Unlike an idol that can neither remind them of the past nor make promises for the future. "Tell us, you idols, what is going to happen. Tell us what the former things were, so that we may consider them and know their final outcome. Or declare to us the things to come, tell us what the future holds, so we may know that you are gods" (Isa. 41:22–23a NIV). But both the people and the calf were blind to the future of all things, and even that was no surprise to God. He knew every inch of that day at the same time He threw the moon into the black, the invention of night. How disappointing their non-transcendent, lifeless, unseeing, and unknowing god would be when asked by Israel, "Where do we go from here, and is there danger there too?": unholy.

Even though their god couldn't be more than what it was, and even though it, ignorant of the future, couldn't know what was to come, Israel still decided to give the calf credit for what happened before its birth. About their golden bull they proclaimed, "These are your gods, O Israel, who brought you up out of the land of Egypt!" (Exod. 32:4). Co-opting God's testimony about Himself, they ascribed the Lord's words and works to a crafted thing that couldn't even save itself from the soon-to-come desecration of its handmade body.

Most likely believing the calf was a representation of Yahweh, as it was with the Egyptians who created idols to image their gods, Israel praised the calf as if it were a messiah. A savior from within their own imagination, despite Moses' witness to who it was that sent him to deliver. "I AM has sent me to you," Moses told the people before the plagues disrupted Egypt's entire world. God's self-revelation as "I AM" was to say that *He is who He is.* Before time, He was. After time, He will continue to be. Totally independent and uncreated, He is totally unrestrained in His ability to save. In terms of power, because it is derived from within Himself, He doesn't need permission to show Himself strong nor is He desperate for anything outside of Himself to supply it. His power can and will never run dry, whether it be the turning of water into blood, filling up an entire city with as many frogs as there are people, or making nature and the very animals and insects it contains a servant to His will. Giving them permission to break out of the ordinary ways in which they function to show that only the Holy God has complete and inexhaustible power over all creation.

As a sovereign, a supreme ruler, creator of heaven and earth, nothing in heaven or on earth can prevent God from delivering whoever it is that He wants to save. For others, Pharaoh's brick-hard heart and the resources he'd maintained and grown on the backs of the oppressed would be for them a signal to retreat. To neglect so great a salvation out of the realization that they, the wannabe savior, didn't have any advantages over Pharaoh so as to overcome him, setting all those under him free. But what is a hard heart to the God who made it? What is an oppressive government with all of its money, chariots, soldiers, and slaves to the God who removes and sets up kings whenever it pleases Him to do so (Dan. 2:21)? God has said, "Is my hand shortened, that it cannot redeem? Or have I no power to deliver?" (Isa. 50:2). To respond with anything other than "no" would be to make God just as impotent as the calf Israel made for themselves. The Holy God's sovereign rule gives Him the ability to use people and circumstances for the purposes of salvation instead of salvation being thwarted by them.

Fast-forward to Christ, who from a human perspective, might've looked like a victim who would succumb to the power and might of the Jewish leaders. However, the circumstances to which they instigated and curated weren't without God's sovereign knowledge or allowance. Peter, reminded of how God used wicked people to accomplish His purpose, said, "Truly in this city there were gathered together against your holy servant Jesus, whom you anointed, both Herod and Pontius Pilate, along with the Gentiles and the peoples of Israel, *to do whatever your hand and your plan had predestined to take place*" (Acts 4:27–28, emphasis added). Jesus didn't primarily fall victim to the schemes of an evil government. Instead, He was a willing participant in the plot God ordained before the world was even formed. We should never expect an unholy thing that was made with our bare hands to be sovereign enough or powerful enough to save us from anything when an idol's entire existence is dependent on whoever it is that brought them to life.

I must also add that for there to be salvation at all, there must also be a holy personhood in the being that does the saving. The golden calf might've had ears on the side of its face. A mouth chiseled right above its jaw. And it could be that even the top of its head was rounded to simulate the presence of a brain beneath its horns, but even with all of the outward symbols of a living being, it was as dead as a ghost. It is ridiculously futile to trust in an idol for deliverance for the sole reason that idols aren't alive. The psalmist's description proves this point: "Their idols are silver and gold, the work of human hands. They have mouths, but *do not speak;* eyes, but *do not see.* They have ears, but *do not hear;* noses, but *do not smell.* They have hands, but *do not feel;* feet, but *do not walk;* and they *do not make a sound* in their throat" (Ps. 115:4–7, emphasis added). If the golden calf did in fact bring them "out of the land of Egypt," how did it know they were enslaved if he didn't have the mind to comprehend it? Maybe it could've learned about their affliction if it had the ears to hear their prayers toward heaven, but nope, a dead thing is deaf too. Let's say that there were no prayers said, but the oppression was observed. Maybe then the calf would know the context for that which its worshipers needed deliverance from; but sadly, it didn't have the eyes to see them or their problems either.

The Holy transcendent God who revealed Himself as "I AM" is truly alive, for as I've said and will say again, He has life in Himself. If God were created, He wouldn't be God, for one thing, but His life would also be a derivative of someone else's, something the "I AM WHO I AM" cannot be. R. C. Sproul says it better than me: "A necessary being is a being who cannot *not* be. It exists by the sheer necessity of its eternal being, of its aseity. . . . God must have the power of being within Himself that is not derived from something outside of Himself. This is transcendent being."[3]

Jesus said that He is "the way, the truth, and *the life*" and that He is "the resurrection and *the life*" (John 14:6; 11:17, emphasis added). We exist only because He does. And we will continue to exist because He will too. Unlike an idol whose life is completely imaginary. It is the faith that we give to an idol that gives it the life that we hope it will give us in return. Paul said to the folks in Corinth, ". . . we know that 'an idol has no real existence,'" and that 'there is no God but one.' . . . yet for us there is one God, the Father, from whom are all things and for whom we exist, and one Lord, Jesus Christ, through whom are all things and through whom we exist" (1 Cor. 8:4, 6). This is an important truth to know and then believe because it is the reason why God is *able* to save or do anything at all.

A god with no life could not notice you in your room, listen to the quiet suffering stuck in your chest, and comprehend it as pain. An idol can't speak so it can neither rebuke

---

[3] R. C. Sproul, *Moses and the Burning Bush* (Sanford, FL: Reformation Trust Publishing, 2018), 81.

or comfort when the time calls for it. And if our idols are mere men, they may have eyes to see and mouths to speak to the issues of your heart, but what they say and what they see will always be narrow compared to God, who doesn't need to call you to know how you are. If God were not a real and living being, all of the dying that happens below Him would not move Him to act because He would not be able to move or, at the very least, feel. God's salvation is God's compassion at work, and God's being is the eye of the tornado of His kindness, a wild but intentional wind coming for the ones hoping that He heard them asking for help. God's salvation of Israel was preceded by God's *awareness* of their needs. He said, "I have surely *seen* the affliction of my people who are in Egypt and have *heard* their cry because of their taskmasters. I *know* their sufferings, and I have *come down* to deliver them out of the hand of the Egyptians" (Exod. 3:7–8, emphasis added). To speak of God is to speak of a being who exists, who is alive at all times and completely attentive to the sin and suffering of all people. An idol's lifelessness makes it ignorant and incapable of serving anyone by way of salvation. To hope in anything that has been made to be a deliverer, whether it's sex, a relationship, a job, money, an identity, alcohol, or whatever is to become as ignorant as the idol itself. "They have no knowledge who carry about their wooden idols, and keep on praying to a god that cannot save" (Isa. 45:20). Another trait of idols that we'd do well to pay attention to is the way the moral compass of anyone who worships them swings. When idols are made, collected, given attention, trusted, or loved, their integrity or ethical standards are rarely what qualifies them as worthy of our faith. The golden calf was invented and then expected to *do* something holy for Israel as opposed to being. Its value was contingent upon its ability to act on their behalf. Never is it mentioned by them in their initial planning of it or praise upon its completion that the calf was a *holy* one, and isn't that something? That every idol Israel or we gather to ourselves is a lawless one? With a standard that's easy enough to be kept and obeyed? Made by our own hands, idols image us in their godlessness, and this is one reason we follow them. Because with all worship, there is a sacrifice, of course, but with idols, the demands that are made don't take an incarnation, death, nor resurrection for us to give it. There are no miracles involved in our obedience to an unholy god because what they require of us, we need no help to yield. Not only that, whatever it is that we offer up to these so-called gods, in praise or petition, is almost always against God's moral law, further exposing the wicked nature of them all. To worship an idol, the exclusive worship reserved for God and God alone is given to an unworthy thing, and to the sometimes surprise of the idol's lover, what they get in exchange isn't the peace they bargained for, but the judgment they've stored up for themselves instead.

Idol worship surely leads to futility of thought and the darkening of the mind's ability to understand, but I am thankful that we are not completely left to ourselves to find out if an idol can be what we've asked of it. There are enough passages that have done that work for us, as we've seen. The work of telling us a truth that we need a resurrection to believe. Idols are never praised for granting wishes. No matter how many candles we blow, fingers we twist, or stars we converse with, an idol will never be able to give us what we truly need and this is why the Scriptures have told us over and again how they "do not profit" (Prov. 11:4; Isa. 44:9; Jer. 2:8; 23:32). Whether you have recognized it or not, I've tried to make the point, maybe too subtle to be seen, that their unprofitability is rooted in their unholiness. Their failure to be God. To be transcendent. Different. To exist in the way we need them to. As a living being, able to see, hear, act, and think. Powerful enough to overcome every power and problem that the world has either inherited or borrowed. *Every idol is a created thing.* For Israel it was a calf without a name, but eventually Baal, Asheroth, or Molech (2 Kings 21:3; Judg. 2:10–23; Jer. 32:35; Lev. 18:21).

Knowing how idolatry functioned in history may lead us to believe that it doesn't exist now. Baal may have died along with the folks that gave him "life," but that primitive form of idolatry has in fact been transferred to us by way of our nature, and evolved into another less obvious version of the same. What might've been Baal once is now sexual identity, sex, autonomy, intellect, relationships, money, marriage, legalism, politics, power, ethnicity, food, social media, children, or whatever other made thing you can think of. We take what God called good and remove a letter. Give it ultimate status in our lives and hope with all of our hearts it will be the deity that we've baptized it as.

I don't know your idols by name. You might, and the God you've exchanged it for certainly does, but know that who or whatever it is, it will fail you forever. I don't say that to shame you, but to come for and against the lies that brought your own golden calf into being. It was manufactured on purpose and eventually trusted to be and do what it can't. Whatever that thing might be, it too is local. Your needs transcend places, and God forbid you have to wait to buy, or call, or fly, or walk to, or knock on the door of a person, place, or thing to get hope or peace or joy. When God, who is both in heaven and in you is already there—where you are—with Himself to give. In Him is life, and ain't we all needy of it? Of Him? Not only for salvation but also satisfaction. Idols function as a kind of "savior."[4] A manufactured messiah made to fill the empty parts within. But if a made thing didn't make you then it surely can't make you whole. Watch and pray that your hope doesn't look to the high places as rescue (Lev. 26:30; Num. 33:52). Instead, look to the hills from where your holy help comes (Ps. 121:1–2), for any other hope is an unholy one.

It's this hope, this unholy faith that I'm hoping to redirect, but let's refresh our memories again by speaking to faith's place in Israel's story. Remember that after creating the golden calf, they wanted the calf to lead them in the way they should go. A holy hope to have indeed but a foolish one to place on a piece of art that can't move nor navigate itself, let alone a community of people. We've trusted our idols to be holy in that way too, of course. To do what only an uncreated, independent being can do. The problem is that with anything that has a beginning, it's automatically limited in what it has to offer. I suspect that this is why when God spoke of His people committing two evils,

---

[4] In his book *Counterfeit Gods*, Tim Keller comments that "biblical texts . . . spell out idolatry as self-salvation." His observation on page 160 of his book influenced my own (New York: Penguin Books, 2009).

that He used the "fountain of living waters" as a metaphor for Himself and "broken cisterns that can hold no water" as a description for Israel's idols (Jer. 2:13). Each idol, a cistern, is able to provide some semblance of life, as if it were godlike in its ability to offer us some measure of good. A little water here, a little water there. This is most likely the reason we think our idols have been good to us. The relationship does provide some comfort. The direct deposit does give some sense of security. Just as the one who fashioned the idol from wood was able to get warmth and cook food from the wood he'd cut (Isa. 44:15), so maybe some of the faith we put in our unholy gods is because we hope, in vain, that what they've given us, they have more of. But this is the thing: in the very construction of the cistern, as in all things not named God, is brokenness. The little water, life, love, affirmation, provision, pleasure it poured out has an end, and as a matter of fact, it was never the source of all this goodness in the first place. All that it gave out came from God's hand, so anybody who has ever praised an idol for its love was actually giving their "thank you" away to the wrong person (Rom. 1:21).

As the "fountain of living waters" God presents Himself as being the only real, true, and lasting source and fulfiller of our continual needs. In Alexander MacClaren's exposition of this text he stated, "God is the fountain of living waters; in other words, in fellowship with God there is full satisfaction for all the capacities and desires of the soul."[5] A point within Scripture that is made over and over again as inspired by the Spirit of the Holy One is that there is an eternity's worth of contrast between God and idols. Idols are said to be useless, unable to deliver, unprofitable, nothing, silent, without life, speechless, blind, unmoving, and empty. By faith, prompted by blindness and utter delusion, all those who worship idols trust them to be the opposite of what they really are. Lifting their eyes to things that have been made, from whence cometh their hell, idol-lovers trade what is true about God in exchange for a lie. As it happens, what remains true about God is not believed, and the essence and attributes of the Creator (holy transcendence and moral purity) are eventually projected onto the creation. Completely blind to reality, we reckon the idol as valuable, God as invaluable. The idol as useful, God as useless. The idol as messiah, God as foe. For what other reason do we choose anything over God if isn't because we think *it* and not *Him* can give us what we need? How often have we looked to the creature and called it Savior, without

---

[5] Alexander MacLaren, *Alexander MacLaren's Expositions of Holy Scripture, Isaiah and Jeremiah* (Public Domain), 245, commentary on Jeremiah 2:13, https://www.studylight.org /commentaries/eng/mac/jeremiah-2.html.

words, but by faith? For every empty bottle of wine, drunk to the dredges without self-control's restraint, there is the proof of a soul wanting to find peace in something that doesn't have it to give.

Even social media thrives most on our neediness and the way it makes us discontent in being known and loved by God and God alone. Looking to *it* and not *Him* for love and other things, every post reveals from what place we find value and identity. Speaking of identity, we were given one from birth, but being an image-bearer is never enough when our faith is not in the One whose image we are made. The knowledge of who we are as an image-bearer testifies to who we were made for, beckoning us to worship Someone more supreme than ourselves. In the exchange of the truth about God for the lie that social media can become, every "like" feels like praise, every comment feels like prayer, and every follow feels like heaven, one that we have constructed to the glory of our own name. It's given us a way to feel as if we know everything, mimicking omniscience. And by giving us access into the hearts (by way of words), lives, families, jobs, finances, past and present of anyone with a page for themselves, we are able to experience a lesser form of omnipresence. Do you find it odd that the way we have chosen to cope with our humanity is by attempting to rise above it? To build the Tower of Babel with the fruit we were commanded not to eat, climb to the top, peek into the heavens and declare ourselves god? On the surface, the idol looks like social media, at the root, the idol is *us.*

Whenever we trust anything other than the holy God to save us from all of our fears, doubts, and anxieties, satisfy our deepest longings, and provide our every need, we have trusted in an unholy god to be what it never will. To say that God is holy is to say that God is God and there is no other God besides Him. "There is none holy like the LORD: for there is none besides you; there is no rock like our God" (1 Sam. 2:2). And if He is the only God, then Elijah's words to Israel ring true for us today: "How long will you go limping between two different opinions? If the LORD is God, follow him; but if Baal, then follow him" (1 Kings 18:21). What point was Elijah trying to make by appealing to the true nature of Yahweh and Baal as the motivating factor for which one should be followed? It's that if a being is indeed God, then He is not only deserving of the exclusivity of our worship, but He is also the only one sufficient for our needs.

Again, idols are described as "useless" and "unprofitable," which speaks to why it's completely futile to think they can do and be what we expect of them. If salvation, they have no power. If resurrection, they have no life. If peace, they don't have the sovereign control of today's circumstances or the divine power to settle anybody's heart when enduring them. If compassion, they have no eyes to see or ears to hear, or mouth to speak; therefore they lack the personhood needed to meet you where you are or to take you where you need to go.

But if we redirect our faith onto the true and living God, in Christ, we will find in Him everything we need. If salvation, He is "mighty to save" (Zeph. 3:17). If resurrection, He is "the resurrection and the life" (John 11:25). If peace, He is "the LORD" who can "bless his people with peace" (Ps. 29:11). If compassion, He is "the LORD . . . a compassionate and gracious God" whose mercies are "new every morning" (Ps. 86:15; Lam. 3:23 NIV). With God comes all that the mind needs for wisdom, all that the heart needs for love, all that the body needs for satisfaction, and all that the affections need for joy. Since Scripture declares that we were not only made by Him but for Him (Col. 1:16), it should be no surprise then that we will never be whole without Him. More than that, if everything good exists because of Him, then there is nothing that exists that is better than Him. As Stephen Charnock would put it, "No man can possibly form a notion of God in his mind and yet form a notion of something better than God; for whoever thinks anything better than God fancieth a God with some defect; by how much the better he thinks that thing to be, by so much the more imperfect he makes God in his thoughts."[6]

In Paul's letter to the Philippians, he says, "Indeed, I count everything as loss because of the surpassing worth of knowing Christ Jesus my Lord. For his sake I have suffered the loss of all things and count them as rubbish, in order that I may gain Christ" (Phil. 3:8). I do hope that you understand what he is claiming. That there is nothing that he has had or will have that he will not give up for Christ, and that once it is all gone, whether put to death by his will, or reckoned dead by his faith, not a single thing that he has lost will ever compare to the God he has gained. This is the significant reality that sets the nature of God at odds with idols, and I hope the motivation needed for you never to exchange Him with another ever again. With idols, they are completely empty and invaluable; but with Christ, He is infinitely valuable with supreme worth. Idolatry is all about exchanging God for what is no god at all, but the kind of faith that Paul describes here is also a trade, if you will. The difference is that it's the exchanging of worthlessness for the Worthy One. The unprofitable for ultimate gain.

---

[6] Stephen Charnock, *Discourses upon the Existence and Attributes of God*, volumes 1–2 (New York: Robert Carter & Brothers, 1874), 216–17.

Broken cisterns for a fountain of living water. A broken heart for one recaptured by God (Ezek. 14:5). Which gives us hope. If we have traded God for an idol, we are not left to ourselves, away from His compassion or help. We can trade back. This is called *repentance*—turning from a dead idol to follow the God who not only has life in Himself but more than enough to share with you. Think about it: if all you have is idols and nothing more, you'd have nothing at all. If all you have is Christ and nothing else, you have everything. Who needs a golden calf when you can have the living God?

Chapter 5

ᚼoly Justice

STARTING A GOSPEL PRESENTATION with "Do you know that you're a sinner?" is the wrong way to begin. Sinners may very well know that they are such because of their conscience or religious memories, but they will not know why being one should terrify them into silence. When sharing that good, good news, we should—dare I say *must*—begin with "Did you know that God is holy?" As you travel through the story, then, venturing into necessary subjects like sin and judgment, God is the context by which both land. If God were not holy, sin wouldn't be sin. All behavior would be non-moral, existing without ethical boundaries. And in a strange way, all that is done under the sun would be impersonal since there wouldn't be a "god" in heaven who could discern the moral difference between murder and music, finding no offense with either. Unbothered with humanity's actions, none of them, no matter how hideous (or not), could shake the smile from his face or nudge him toward justice. He'd sit there, in that unholy heaven, while chaos went on beneath him, as time moved every wicked (or not) person, place, or thing toward an eternity without consequences.

What I imagined above is as mythological as a fairy. If we let the unredeemed tell it, an unrighteous God is preferable, but they have no say-so in the matter anyhow. With God, "all his ways are justice. A God of faithfulness and without iniquity, just and upright is he" (Deut. 32:4). A fact we've digested by now. That our God is a morally pure one. But does that require Him to be a vengeful one? Well, if He is as righteous as Scripture describes Him to be, then the answer must be "yes."

Some of the work that's needed in grappling with the justice of God is coming to terms with how a holy God interacts with sin. Habakkuk told us that God's eyes are too pure to look at evil or to tolerate wrongdoing (1:13). An unsightly vision it must be. "He cannot look on sin without loathing it; he cannot look on sin but his heart riseth against it; it must be most odious to him as that which is against the glory of his nature and directly opposite to that which is the luster and varnish of all his other perfections."[1]

---

[1] Stephen Charnock, *Discourses upon the Existence and Attributes of God,* volumes 1–2 (New York: Robert Carter & Brothers, 1874), 181.

When God sees sin in all of its different colors, He doesn't see Himself, He being most beautiful. There is nothing so unlike God than sin. Nothing so awful as that presence within us that is repelled by God's voice. God's holiness recognizes sin as it is. A foreigner without glory. Sickening at its core, vomit by another name. The root of ungodly behavior. The reason creation images the devil in its defiance of a better love. There is in it the constant attempt to masquerade itself like it's another version of the Lord, hoping we won't pick up on the stench of deceit, and sadly, apart from the Holy Spirit's intervention, we never do.

As common as sin is for all of us—for every descendent of Adam apart from Jesus—it does not and cannot exist in God. God's righteousness, an "ethical dimension of His holiness" means that all that God does is right.[2] Someone may ask, "What is the *right* thing to do and who defines it?" A worthwhile question, in fact, considering the world and the many, many ideas it has regarding good and evil, which are most often determined by affection and not faith. Sin deludes folks into thinking that their feelings and creaturely thoughts hold weight in our moral universe as

---

[2] Fred Zaspel, "Four Aspects of Divine Righteousness," Reformation & Revival Journal, vol. 6, no. 4, Winter 1997.

if God is not the ultimate authority on goodness. We can know if something is right by whether or not it conforms to God's character; therefore, God is righteous because He cannot deviate from His own standard as communicated in His law. And lest you think God borrowed a set of rules from another and obligated Himself to it, know that that's impossible. There is no moral authority higher than God. God Himself is the standard by which all right and wrong is determined. Which is to say that whatever is good morally is whatever is like God. "Everything in the universe is good to the degree it conforms to the nature of God and evil as it fails to do so" said Tozer.[3] So, when Scripture tells us that God is a righteous God, it is saying that God is true to Himself in regard to moral purity. Every deed, word, and thought with God is without spot, wrinkle or blemish. Fred Zaspel remarked, "When Scripture declares that God does what is right, it affirms merely that He faithfully adheres to His own perfections. He acts only and always according to the very highest principle of justice: Himself."[4]

---

[3] A. W. Tozer, *The Knowledge of the Holy* (New York: HarperCollins, 1978), 68.

[4] Fred Zaspel, "Four Aspects of Divine Righteousness," *Reformation & Revival Journal*, volume 6, number 4, Winter 1997.

Which still leaves us with the question: what does God's righteousness have to do with God's justice? Clearly, some people of the earth have spoken and have given us their own explanation of how God deals with sinners. In an attempt to justify their belief that God isn't antagonistic toward sin, there are those that will say, "God is love." They most likely don't realize it but what they're ultimately claiming is that God is unjust. In their defense, the veil that covers, darkening their wisdom, keeps them from seeing their argument as theologically illogical (Rom. 1:21; Eph. 4:17–19; 2 Cor. 3:14; 4:4). To them, love must be lenient or at least compassionate, which to them means setting aside all offenses so that God may be allowed to dispense forgiveness to anyone who needs it.

Ironically, what they wrongly suspect of God is what they'll rightly protest when observed in a person. Have we not seen that holy rage that rises in us when a brown boy is murdered and he, and not the one who threw the bullet, is blamed for it? When he, the murderer, goes without an indictment, a sentence of guilt, or some judicial consequence for throwing his bullets at an innocent body, don't we lament? Don't we tell justice to stop hiding? And where do you think we got it from—that sense of knowing the scales should be balanced? You'd be telling the truth if you traced the desire for equilibrium back to God. For we all testify to His image in us when we expect justice to "roll down like water" (Amos 5:24). We *know* almost instinctively that the guilty must be punished until the guilty one is us.

God's "rectoral righteousness," as the fancy theologians call it, is that aspect of God's righteousness that imposes laws on every man and woman made, requiring from them righteousness in return. When God says, "Love Me" (see Matt. 22:37), it isn't a request but a command of the highest order. It is God legislating glory, worship, and honor for Him alone, outlawing idolatry, the sin that begets all others. When God says, "Love your neighbor," it too isn't an arbitrary suggestion to which we have the right to ignore, but it is a law obligating humanity to love one another as God Himself does. In essence, in obedience to God's law, we are imaging God in His righteousness, being holy as He is (Lev. 11:44).

But what happens when we don't obey? When God says, "Love Me," and we stiffen our necks? When God says, "Love your neighbor," and we creatures take it upon ourselves to let hate be our lord? What is required of a righteous God when His law is broken, His truth is not sought, His wisdom is not esteemed, His beauty is not treasured, His goodness is not savored, His promises are not believed, His holiness not reverenced, and everything that makes God God is not loved?[5] Once Abraham asked, "Shall not the judge of all the earth do what is just?" or in another translation, "Will not the Judge of all the earth do *right?*" (Gen. 18:25 NIV, emphasis added). If God be holy, He must be just, and in so doing, He must punish sinners. In God's self-revelation, He has made it known that He will by no means clear the guilty (Num. 14:18).

For our benefit, as an example and perhaps proof of God's righteous judgment of sinners, the Scriptures have recorded more than enough evidence of His wrath. When the Lord saw an earth happy with its own wickedness, He set His face against it. He promised to bring a flood that left everybody and everything that had breath without it. The transcendent God reigned above their ability to hide their thoughts from each other. Unlike their neighbors wrapped in flesh, God saw every quiet rebellion. He heard every silent treason, and because of it, He flooded the earth leaving only one family to mourn. When God saw the many, many sins done in the city of Sodom, He hated it (Pss. 5:5; 11:5; 45:7). Yes, hate. "If he should for one instant cease to hate [sin], he would cease to live. To be a

---

[5] Adapted from John Piper, "What Is Sin? The Essence and Root of All Sinning," February 2, 2015; https://www.desiringgod.org/messages/what-is-sin-the-essence-and-root-of-all-sinning.

holy God, is as essential to him, as to be a living God."⁶ Oh, how offended our God must've been when He looked at Sodom and Gomorrah and didn't see Himself in how they lived. Everybody's body in that city (and ours) was made for a higher, more glorious purpose than the perversion to which it was subjected. What defiance it is to use the body God gave as an altar for our own glory? Every act of sexual immorality, apathy toward the poor, and arrogance was a curse word thrown at heaven (Gen. 13:13; 18:20–21; Ezek. 16:49–50; Jude 7;. And in response, from heaven came fire (Gen. 19:1–29).

The garden of Eden branded with perfection from its birth was a witness to God's command and eventual judgment of Adam. "In the day you eat of it, you *will* surely die" said God, and die Adam did (Gen. 2:17; 5:5). His wickedness was a decision he himself made. No one held a gun to his head forcing him to eat what God had forbidden, but his heart opened his mouth and out of it came the word "shoot." That's a metaphor for how we, like Adam, choose our fate. Sin separates, creating distance between God and what He's made, which is one of the motivations of the sinner, to stiff-arm God.

---

⁶ Charnock, *Discourses upon the Existence and Attributes of God*, volumes 1–2, 181.

Idolators don't want the real God; they want to *be* Him. With all of their might they work to have some sort of distance between them and their maker, constructing an alternate reality in which they are their own lord and king and unbeknownst to them, God lifts His hand to give them exactly what their heart desires. This too is judgment. A wrath that Paul says is being revealed from heaven against all ungodliness, relaxing the gracious restraints that keep us from doing what "ought not to be done" (Rom. 1:18, 28). What do I mean? That one form of God's judgment is to simply give us over to what we want. J. I. Packer's framing of this is helpful: "Scripture sees hell as self-chosen. . . . All receive what they actually chose, either to be with God forever, worshiping him, or without God forever, worshiping themselves."[7] Adam decided he wanted death instead of God, and his wish was granted.

When it came time to return the ark of the covenant to its place in Jerusalem, it was set on a cart. A deadly mistake that would soon cost a man his life. According to the law, the ark was to be carried on the shoulders of the Levites with poles (Lev. 7:9). Instead of referring to God's Word for how to handle God's stuff, Uzzah and others took

---

[7] J. I. Packer, *Concise Theology* (Carol Stream, IL: Tyndale, 1993), 262–63.

their cues from the Philistines. An ignorant act for them, doing what they knew not of. But these men, the descendants of Abraham, knew how to know better. They went along with the ark seemingly settled on a cart, as songs moved in between the people of God translating Israel's joy while the cymbals clapped like God was coming home. Then it happened. Upon reaching the threshing floor, the oxen forgot its legs and started to dip near the ground. The ark, that precious symbol of God's holy, holy, holy presence tilted, threatening the dirt to catch it. As it did, Uzzah extended his hand to grab the ark by the hand in an attempt to keep it in its place, and according to the text, "the anger of the LORD was kindled against Uzzah, and God struck him down there because of his error, and he died there beside the ark of God" (2 Sam. 6:7).

We feel sorry for Uzzah, don't we? From our perspective, he was simply a man with good intentions. A man who just wanted to keep the ark from meeting the ground. The reach of his hand toward the ark looks like a fruit of the Spirit—a kind gesture. Uzzah was just trying to *help*, we say. Help, huh? It's interesting the words we use to describe things. No wonder we're so confused by judgment at times. We're too busy giving bad things good names. Scripture calls Uzzah's actions "error" which the NIV translates as "irreverent act." Either name gets at the reason for his death. Uzzah sinned against God. Maybe thinking himself holy enough to touch what he shouldn't or because it had been in his father's home for two decades, the ark had become too common. An ornament of sorts. The holy, holy, holy God should never be treated as so familiar to the degree that He becomes approachable on our own terms, but as we see with Uzzah, his loss of awe paired with his failure to do what God's law prescribed necessitated God's justice. Now don't get me wrong; I am not supposing that Uzzah's actions were purposely malicious or lacking sincerity. He was acting on instinct out of what he might've believed was respect. But even if seemingly natural and sincere, such was forbidden. When the ark began to slip, his impulse was to keep it above ground, but as R. C. Sproul put it: "Uzzah assumed that his hand was less polluted than the earth."[8]

Whenever God judges like this, the dead body with a "helpful" hand, a reminiscent wife turned to salt (Gen. 19:26), a man and his family swallowed whole by the untrustworthy ground on which they stood (Num. 16:32), an entire city devoted to destruction including all of its men and women and the babies they labored for (Josh. 6:17;

---

[8] R. C. Sproul, *The Holiness of God* (Carol Stream, IL: Tyndale, 1985), 108.

1 Sam. 15:3), we don't know what to think. We are tempted to be like David, who was angry "because the LORD had broken out against Uzzah" (2 Sam. 6:8). It confuses us that the same God who is praised for His kindness can seem so cruel. So easily given to rage, supposedly.

As He is transcendent and thus different, incomparable, God's wrath is nothing like the anger we know of by experience. Wrath isn't a response to God's ego being bruised nor is it that He's a sadist, taking pleasure in our pain. It is quite the opposite. The wrath of God is the "holy revulsion of God's being against that which is a contradiction to his holiness."[9] God cannot be indifferent toward sin because He is too holy, holy, holy to do so. It is true that "[God's] justice is the great witness to his purity"[10] for if He were to overlook the guilty, no matter how small the offense may be, He would be unjust. Unholy then. If we saw sin as God does, we would say along with the angels, "Just are you, O Holy One, who is and who was, for you brought these judgments. For they have shed the blood of saints and prophets, and you have given them blood to drink. It is what they deserve!" (Rev. 16:5–6).

---

[9] John Murray, *The Epistle to the Romans* (Grand Rapids: Wm. B. Eerdmans, 1968), 35.

[10] Charnock, *Discourses upon the Existence and Attributes of God*, volumes 1–2, 182.

The reason we empathize with the likes of Uzzah and eventually find the confidence to accuse God of injustice whenever His gavel falls too hard for our liking is because we have a ridiculously low view of sin and an equally mediocre grasp of the holiness of God. He is without spot. He is without wrinkle. He is without blemish. Sin is different. It is offensive, abominable, demonic, unrighteous, lawless. Sin will never have His heart or His ways, and out of His purity He has delivered a law to all men that if obeyed, they would be just as beautiful as He is, but they will not allow it. So then, God must do what is right; He must judge. He must lift His sword and bring it down on the guilty (2 Sam. 24:16–17; 1 Chron. 21:16).

But here's the question that *should* be asked but rarely is: If God *must* judge, why am I *still* alive? Haven't I eaten a fruit that God told me not to? Haven't I made my body an altar? Haven't I ignored the "least of these" and used something silly to justify my apathy? Haven't I become too familiar with the Holy One, laying my reverence aside while maintaining the perception of faithfulness. I mean, aren't we all guilty then (Rom. 3:11, 23)? Not just you and me, but everyone alive has sinned against God, falling short of His glory; and yet, here we are. Still under the sun, reading a book, a common grace. A joy given to men who deserve nothing but wrath.

Similar to Uzzah becoming too familiar with the ark, we are so used to the patience of God that we are more stunned by His judgments than we are by His forbearance. As R. C. Sproul said, "The issue is not why does God punish sin but why does He permit the ongoing human rebellion? It is customary or usual for God to be forbearing. He is indeed long-suffering, patient, and slow to anger. In fact, He is so slow to anger that when His anger does erupt, we are shocked and offended by it."[11] We are the guilty ones to which God must judge, but He has not given us what we deserve, yet. A mercy.

For every story where there is wrath, there are even more stories with mercy. Consider Adam and how after the chewing, an animal was killed, blood spilled, its skin stripped from its body and made into a covering for the accursed ones (Gen. 3:21). An act not asked for, but one that God initiated and took care of Himself. Before fire from heaven came down to make a flame out of everyone alive in Sodom, the angels came for Lot, to rescue him. The basis for it wasn't his own righteousness—the lack thereof is evident in him being willing to throw his daughters to the wolves (Gen. 19:4–8). Even as the heavens began to open up wide, making room for God's wrath to fall, Lot lingered

---

[11] Sproul, *The Holiness of God*, 117.

as if to show his lack of urgency and perhaps lack of reverence toward the grace of God. He too should've been burned to dust, but the angels grabbed him and his family by the hand, snatching them into safety not because they deserved it, but because mercy met him at the door (Gen. 19:16–17).

Or consider Egypt, when God made it His business to judge Egypt for its idolatry by coming for their firstborn everything, the angel of death flew right on by any home with blood on its posts. Let us remember that the bright red blood wasn't Israel's idea. They only knew to do it because God took pleasure in communicating their way of escape. This too was another mercy brought about by God's hand, for Israel was just as deserving of God's justice as the Egyptians. The only difference between the two nations was that God decided to have compassion on one and not the other. God has said of Himself, "I will have mercy on whom I will have mercy, and I will have compassion on whom I will have compassion" (Exod. 33:19 NIV). The holy, holy, holy God owes us nothing, but His compassion is what He's given us anyway. Like David, who stole a man's wife right under his nose, and put him to death to avoid the confession. But of course, God saw the theft, the pride, the fornication, the abuse of power, and how it made a woman have to mourn her husband while nursing his murderer's child. The good thing is that David confessed, finally. "I have sinned against the LORD," he said. The troublesome thing is, he didn't die because of it. "The LORD also has put away your sin; you shall not die," Nathan said to David, the guilty king, whose condemnation was warranted (2 Sam. 12:13).

The Lord put away David's sin, Nathan said. Put it where, though? On a guiltless animal, maybe? An unblemished one that was then taken and slaughtered in David's place? Atoning for what he'd done right under God's nose? If so, this too wouldn't be enough to justify him being pardoned, seeing that "it is impossible for the blood of bulls and goats to take away sins" (Heb. 10:4). If the sacrificial system itself wasn't good enough to atone for sin and placate God's wrath, then what is there to say about God when He decided to be merciful to the guilty? God cannot be as holy as He claims if He allows the guilty to go free. Whether it's Adam or David, Israel or us, to put away our sin without enacting justice on it would be for God to make Himself just as unrighteous as we are. And isn't that what the world presents God as when they expect Him to forgive without justice or be merciful without condemnation? Isn't it that they want a God who is so indifferent toward His glory that He would lay aside His righteousness (if possible) so that He could declare a child of the devil innocent? What an unholy God He would be, but that is the predicament that God was in by passing over the former sins (Mic. 7:18). This is the great dilemma of heaven.

The mercy God displayed toward all who sinned before Christ begs the question of how can God be merciful and righteous at the same time? John Piper posed a good question around this point: "How many wrestle with the apparent injustice that God is lenient with sinners? Indeed, how many Christians wrestle with the fact that our own forgiveness is a threat to the righteousness of God?"[12] I've said this already, but it bears repeating; if God is holy, God must be just. So then, what did the holy God do to make sure that He could offer us forgiveness while not compromising His own righteousness? Obviously the bloodied door post and spotless lamb would be insufficient to totally redeem us. From His hand, what good gift did God the Father give to the world out of love?

God gave His Son, the only One good enough to appease God's wrath. The innocent One taking on the burdens of the guilty so that when forgiveness was dispensed, God's righteousness would be upheld. "For there is no distinction: for all have sinned and fall short of the glory of

---

[12] John Piper, "The Just and the Justifier," May 23, 1999, https://www.desiringgod.org/messages/the-just-and-the-justifier.

God, and are justified by his grace as a gift, through the redemption that is in Christ Jesus, whom God put forward as a propitiation by his blood, to be received by faith. *This was to show God's righteousness, because in his divine forbearance he had passed over former sins. It was to show his righteousness at the present time, so that he might be just and the justifier of the one who has faith in Jesus"* (Rom. 3:22–26, emphasis added). Hallelujah.

If anyone took God's kindness toward the sinners of old seriously, they'd have the right to accuse God of injustice. But the cross of Christ was a demonstration not merely of love, as we rightly proclaim with ease, but of justice. He did not leave the guilty unpunished, but instead, their sins and ours were assigned to the spotless Son of God and on Him, God's justice fell. Scripture says that "for our sake he made him to be sin who knew no sin . . ." (2 Cor. 5:21). And when He did, when He looked upon His Son and saw the wickedness Jesus bore, the abominations He took on, the perversions He held in His hand, the rebellion that covered Him, in God the Father rose a holy rage toward the Son He loved. The cup the Son so desperately wanted to pass from Him, full of wrath, of holy hatred, was poured out. "For in the hand of the LORD there is a cup with foaming wine, well mixed, and he pours out from it, and all the wicked of the earth shall drain it down to the dregs" (Ps. 75:8).

Imagine it, if you can, how the cup tasted. What hell concentrated into three hours felt like on the way down. Like infinite displeasure. Absolute abhorrence. Divine distance. The height of holy indignation. Incomprehensible abandonment. In this, it was the will of the Lord to crush Him underfoot (Isa. 53:10). Underneath the heavy weight of God's wrath, the Son who prior to the cross only knew of His Father's delight now asked Him, "My God, my God, why have you forsaken me?" (Matt. 27:46). The answer is plain now. The Son was forsaken so that all who are far off may be brought near. So that everyone who has broken God's law may be acquitted. There was no other way for God to be both merciful *and* just, both loving and righteous, unless God sent a substitute. Either the sinner paid for their own sins, receiving no pardon, or the sinner is pardoned by virtue of someone else's payment. Abraham's son was spared from the tip of His father's knife because the Lord provided Him with a ram as replacement. To us, the Lamb of God was given, sparing us from heaven's sword. As always, God has been the origin of mercy. The heavenly dilemma has been solved in Christ Jesus. Now we say with Paul, "Blessed are those whose lawless deeds are forgiven, and whose sins are covered; blessed is the man against whom the Lord will not count his sin" (Rom. 4:7–8). Hallelujah.

At the cross of Calvary was a display of both justice and mercy. The holy God was so committed to the preservation of His righteousness that He would not, as He said, clear the guilty. But He was equally compelled by that love to which He is so full of to be merciful. So much so that His own Son was put forth as a propitiation. This means that Christ's absorption of the wrath of God removes it from all who have faith in Jesus, never to be experienced in this life or the next. All there is left for us is peace—with God, that is.

Please understand the significance of this. That God's hatred of sin didn't keep Him from loving you, but He chose, on His own accord to rescue you from the wrath to come. Do you know that that is what it means to be *saved*? We say that word without definition to the point that I often wonder if we remember that the term is in reference to divine justice. In one place it says, "Since, therefore, we have now been justified by his blood, much more shall we be *saved by him from the wrath of God*" (Rom. 5:9, emphasis added). And in another: ". . . and how you turned to God from idols to serve the living and true God, and to wait for his Son from heaven, whom he raised from the dead, *Jesus who delivers us from the wrath to come*" (1 Thess. 1:9–10, emphasis added).

The good news is just that—good news—because it declares how Jesus' death has dealt with God's wrath, setting sinners free from the penalty awaiting them, delivering them into safety, into right relationship with God where they are now not treated as their sins deserve but are given the right to be called children of God.

Abraham asked God, "Will not the Judge of all the earth do right?" (Gen. 18:25 NIV). The answer is plain now. In Christ, the Judge *has* done what is right. He is both just *and* the justifier of the one who has faith in Jesus. Hallelujah.

Chapter 6

𝔥𝔬𝔩𝔶 𝔥𝔬𝔴?: 𝔥𝔬𝔩𝔶 𝔙𝔦𝔰𝔦𝔬𝔫

THE PURITAN JOHN OWEN defined sanctification as ". . . an immediate work of the Spirit of God on the souls of believers, purifying and cleansing their natures from the pollution and uncleanness of sin, renewing in them the image of God and thereby enabling them from a spiritual and habitual principle of grace, to yield obedience unto God."[1] Sanctification is an important conversation because it deals with the believer becoming more like God. The Spirit of God inspired Peter to say, "As he who called you is holy, you also be holy in all your conduct, since it is written, 'You shall be holy, for I am holy'" (1 Pet. 1:15–16). The writer of Hebrews provides the consequence of failing to pursue

---

[1] *The Works of John Owen,* ed. William H. Goold, vol. 3: *Pneumatologia: A Discourse Concerning the Holy Spirit* (Edinburgh: T&T Clark, n.d.), 386.

this. "Pursue peace with everyone, and holiness—without it no one will see the Lord" (Heb. 12:14 csb).

But before tossing holiness passages your way and challenging you to obey, as many books on the topic have the habit of doing, I believe it's necessary to first establish what holy thing must happen in us before we are even able to be holy ourselves. The agent of this work is the Holy Spirit. To neglect Him in any discussion regarding sanctification is to venture off into a land Scripture hasn't led you to. And a land that Scripture beckons you to flee from. Without the Holy Spirit, any hope of being holy like God is futile.

How people are described before the Holy Spirit does His work is sobering. The language is unflattering, in fact, and intentionally horrific. What is said of us is that we are lovers of darkness, children of wrath with hearts of stone (Ezek. 11:19; 36:26; John 3:19; Eph. 2:3). It sounds like a movie. One of the scary ones with invisible footprints and voices coming from the walls. The kind that the brave ones watch without light, that is, until the shadows keep them from an easy sleep. In cinema there are plenty of images of ghosts and zombies, the beings that were alive once, who've climbed from underneath the ground to walk among the living. They scare us, as they should, because they seem to exist so differently than us, in clothing, skin, voice, and movement; but our similarities are there, beneath the surface. What they are externally is what Scripture describes us as by nature. We too are the dead ones.

Let's use our creative faculties and imagine that someone with more sense than a zombie went up to a body, a dead one, with nothing but good intentions for it. In a tone not too authoritative to seem rude but strong enough to signify its importance they say, "Live!" They watch the body, the fingers, waiting for a twitch, something. Noticing that nothing has changed, the body still cold, unmoving, they try again, but this time they use another word: "Feel!" And then another: "Think!" As an observer, we'd suppose that the living one had gone mad. "Don't they know the person is dead? Don't they see that the only thing a dead body can do is nothing?" It seems obvious enough, but does it surprise you that this scenario describes us when we try to be holy apart from the resurrection power of the Holy Spirit?

In our natural state, Paul describes us as being "dead in trespasses and sins" with a mind that is "hostile to God" that "will not submit to God's law" and cannot for "those who are in the flesh cannot please God" (Eph. 2:1–2; Rom. 8:7–8). And what does that look like exactly? It's simple really. It looks like going through life like God isn't real. Or good. Or right. Or wise. Or true. Or our Maker. Before the Spirit breathes life into us, we love the darkness and everything it creates. We take the body God made and tell it to obey *us* instead. We look our neighbors in the face, ignore God's image in them, and call them by a name God would never say. Our arrogance is a liar to the point that in hell, millions are there who thought heaven would open up wide just because they went to church. Or because they sponsored a child once. Or because they read a holy book before bed. We are so easily deceived, and even then, our hard hearts will stumble upon truth and still treat it like a lie. It is such a heavy stone we have inside. So heavy that if and when we are told how Jesus is the strong one, it or we won't move because we would do anything to keep God from getting too close. Why? Because the sinner's true condition is that they, or better yet, we don't *want* Him and neither do we want to be *like* Him.

The preacher may say, "Live!" And we will not budge. The casket is our home and we are too dead to leave it anyhow. The gospel may beckon us to "Feel" but we can't. The affections are so entrenched in sin, so in love with hell, that they refuse to give their love to God. Sin and not God is where the unregenerate derives their joy. The Scriptures may cry, "Think!" but until God says, "Let there be light," there will not be (2 Cor. 4:6). A dead person's mind can't concern itself with the thoughts of the living, and if it tried—as we do before we are raised—it is unable to accept such things. When we hear something spiritual such as, "If anyone would come after me, let him deny himself and take up his cross daily and follow me" (Luke 9:23), we call it dumb and believe that our assessment of spiritual truths is in fact wisdom. Thinking ourselves to be wise, we become fools (1 Cor. 1:18–27; 3:18; Rom. 1:22). This is typical of what Scripture calls "the natural person," also known as the dead one (1 Cor. 2:14; Eph. 2:15; 4:8). "The natural person does not accept the things of the Spirit of God, for they are folly to him, and he is not able to understand them because they are spiritually discerned" (1 Cor. 2:14). It is not purely because of ignorance that people will not flee to God for forgiveness, but blindness. As the heart is, the mind is too, both darkened and incapable of functioning correctly or behaving righteously (Rom. 1:21).

The complete deadness of the heart and mind is what makes obedience to God's moral law impossible. That is why I refused to begin this chapter with anecdotal suggestions for how to be holy without first addressing why we can't. We already have too many dead folks dressing themselves up in clean clothes and memorizing the language of the living for fun. We are prone to look into God's law with some strange self-confidence, an inner assurance or ego that exaggerates our own abilities, produced by none other than the flesh; the spirit of our age is to work endlessly, excel at everything, and rest never—and we bring that into our quest for holiness. Wanting human methods for maturity, a natural way to be heavenly, our motivations are sadly mistaken. In them, we feel that we can work for holiness when the God-sent prerequisite to our sanctification simply begins with "believe in the one he has sent" (John 6:29 CSB). Make no mistake about it, we have no power in and of ourselves to do what God has required of us. No matter how confident we are or orthodox we think, a power that is independent of us must transform us from the inside out. We must be made alive before we can be made holy.

To be made alive, one must be born again. Just as a dead body can't do anything, a dead nature can't be holy. As it is described in the Scriptures, a stony heart is what prevents us from being like God. It is called that because a stone is a familiar object for everyone above ground. A stone is unfeeling, unresponsive, immovable if a mountain, hard always. The heart is another way to speak of our moral center or the place from which all of our actions have a root. So then, our moral center is as lifeless as a rock. Solomon went after other gods because his heart was turned toward them (1 Kings 11:4), and other evils are born from the same hard place. Jesus told us this: "For out of the heart come evil thoughts, murder, adultery, sexual immorality, theft, false witness, slander" (Matt. 15:19).

And this: "The good person out of the good treasure of his heart produces good, and the evil person out of his evil treasure produces evil, for out of the abundance of the heart his mouth speaks" (Luke 6:45). What fruit would you expect to grow from this kind of ground? Place the seed, water it too, wish it good luck, and wait to see nothing useful come from this work unless the sun hovers over and transforms the rock into soil.

When born again, this is what happens to us. The Spirit that hovered over the face of the waters comes to earth, to the natural man, born of dirt (Gen. 1:2). He doesn't come because He's been invited either, as our songs would have us believe, nor does He move because we've given Him permission. It's become a habit to speak to and of the Spirit as if He is an energy, a force, or a child that is dependent on our words to act. The Spirit of God *is* God; therefore His transcendent nature sets Him apart from us, in turn defining Him as being independent *of us*. The Holy Spirit does what He wants, when He wants, where He wants, and how He wants. Of the Spirit, Jesus said, "The wind blows *where it wishes*, and you hear its sound, but *you do not know where it comes from or where it goes*. So it is with everyone who is born of the Spirit" (John 3:8, emphasis added). The Spirit of God operates in total freedom, as in, He is not constrained by some force outside of

Himself. This may give new meaning to "where the Spirit of the Lord is, there is freedom" (2 Cor. 3:17). So it is with everyone who receives the Spirit; He has provided for them what He has always had.

He does this through the miracle of *regeneration* (Titus 3:5). Which is the supernatural work of the Holy Spirit, granting life to the dead sinner, giving them the ability to exercise faith and new inclinations toward God.[2] To Israel and us, God promised to do this. Through the prophet Ezekiel He said, "And I will give you a new heart, and a new spirit I will put within you. And I will remove the heart of stone from your flesh and give you a heart of flesh. And I will put my Spirit within you, and cause you to walk in my statutes and be careful to obey my rules" (Ezek. 36:26–27). The new birth—the Spirit making a dead heart come to life—is the genesis of our holiness.

In our flesh, we attempt to switch the order from which holiness can be born. Obeying the rules and walking in His statutes does not *make* the Spirit come nor does it regenerate the soul. No one is spiritually born by means of "the will of the flesh" because "that which is born of flesh is flesh" (John 1:13; 3:6). Meaning, we are only able to birth

---

[2] Defintion adapted from "Regeneration: An Essay by Matthew Barrett," https://www.thegospelcoalition.org/essay/regeneration/.

our own kind. We are only able to produce a replica of ourselves. The natural person can only generate a natural person. Even if Eve tried her best to push a new being out of her womb, her sons and their sons and their daughters and their daughter's daughters would share in her depravity. Every baby is a mirror tracing back to Adam. Children fresh out of the womb are only *new* in the sense of not having been in the world before, but none of them are new in the sense of having a different nature than the flesh that brought them forth. We are sinners because our parents are too. Unlike the children who are born of the Spirit, whose first cry is a holy one. What precedes their birth is the implantation of the nature of the holy God where they are given the power of being like God in His righteousness but not the power to be God Himself. The complete reversal of Satan's lie. The original reason we were made, to be human and holy.

At random (it seems), the Spirit meets the dead in a pew, on a bus, in a club, on a corner, a room, wherever—and in an instant, the natural person is made into a spiritual being. You could call it a spontaneous resurrection of the inner person. That stony heart with all of its disordered loves and misaligned loyalties is replaced by a new one made of flesh. The heart of flesh is completely different from the heart of stone in that it is a *true* heart. One that is alive. It can feel and respond. Once this new heart is implanted, the ear hears "live" and the heart of flesh gives blood to the limbs so it can move toward God. The words *feel* and *think* no longer float like birds without a home. Out of Noah's window, they are doves whose feet have a place to land. That new heart has no room for the unholy things it once kept, but by no means does it remain vacant. What the old man once loved is replaced by a higher, more satisfying affection for God. Thomas Chalmers said, speaking of the new birth, "It is then that the heart, brought under the mastery of one great and predominant affection, is delivered from the tyranny of its former desires."[3]

Holiness begins once the old man has died and the new man has come to life (2 Cor. 5:17). Archibald Alexander summed it up: "It can be easily said, in the general that by this change a principle of holiness is implanted, spiritual life is communicated, the mind is enlightened, the will renewed and the affections purified and elevated to heavenly objects."[4] From beginning to end, the Spirit's work is a gift the natural man didn't ask for but one they received anyway.

---

[3] Thomas Chalmers, *The Expulsive Power of a New Affection*, (Wheaton, IL: Crossway, 2020).

[4] Alexander Archibald, *Thoughts on Religious Experience* (Carlisle, PA: Banner of Truth Trust, 1978), 79.

"For by grace you have been saved through faith. And this is not your own doing; it is the gift of God" (Eph. 2:8).

Holy Vision

After making us alive, how then does the Spirit make us holy? First, He gives us holy vision.

With a brand-new heart comes brand-new sight. The veil that stood in the natural man's line of sight since birth is torn in two by the breaking through of divine light. As the darkness fades, Christ is finally seen with brand new eyes, and isn't He beautiful?

I've heard it said that we become what we behold. Of idols and those that worship them, God through the psalmist said, "Their idols are silver and gold, the work of human hands. They have mouths, but do not speak; eyes, but do not see. They have ears, but do not hear; noses, but do not smell. They have hands, but do not feel; feet, but do not walk; and they do not make a sound in their throat. *Those who make them become like them; so do all who trust in them*" (Ps. 115:4–8, emphasis added). To speak of their trust is to also speak of their spiritual eyes and how attentive they are to the things that are made. Seeing is a kind of believing in this case. It is a faith dead to God, yes, but alive to idols. And that faith works to transform the see-er into what he has put his heart's eyes on, so much so that looking to an idol to be what it cannot, eventually transforms the lover into his idol's image. To not hear, not speak, not see, is to share in their idol's deadness, the disposition of the rebellious. "Son of man, you live among rebels *who have eyes but refuse to see. They have ears but refuse to hear.* For they are a rebellious people" (Ezek. 12:2 NLT, emphasis added). Watch a person up close and it won't be long before you can discern who or what she looks at most. If the Creator, you'll see glory. If the creature, you'll see darkness. Our rebellion is rooted in our sinful nature, yes, but what our sinful nature did to our sight is part of the reason we lived as we did.

John made the connection between seeing and sinning when he wrote, "No one who keeps on sinning has either *seen him* or known him" (1 John 3:6, emphasis added). And again, "Whoever does evil has not *seen God*" (3 John 1:11, emphasis added). The statements are perplexing, and to us it may seem like a contradiction when we compare it with Scriptures like, "No one has ever seen or can see him" (1 Tim. 6:16). But there's no need to fret, because the kind of seeing John speaks of is different than the kind of seeing that only Jesus knew of (John 1:18). John's kind of seeing is the same as Paul when he prayed this: "I do not cease to give thanks for you, remembering you in my prayers, that the God of our Lord Jesus Christ, the Father of glory, may give you the Spirit of wisdom and of revelation in the knowledge of him, having *the eyes of your hearts enlightened*, that you may know what is the hope to which he has called you" (Eph. 1:16–18, emphasis added). This kind of sight can only come by way of regeneration. Before we are made to stand above our grave in victory over sin and death, we may have natural eyes to see the sky, our skin, the leaves and how they turn brown before Christmas, but though we may see with those eyes, we don't *see* the glory to be beheld in them, and how they are the evidence that there is a God. God's invisible attributes are clearly perceived or *seen* by the eyes, but not by the heart, and this is to blame for our refusal to honor God as God (Rom. 1:20–21).

To be blind in this way is to not recognize God as the supreme beauty that He is, leading us to live as if everything God has made is more beautiful than Him. That is truly the sin beneath all sins. "What makes our sinful condition so devastating is that we are blind to divine glory—blind to the beauty of Christ in the gospel. We can look right at it when reading it in the Bible, or hearing it preached, or singing it, and we see nothing glorious."[5] This

---

[5] John Piper, "Why Do Christians Preach and Sing?" January 3, 2015; https://www.desiringgod.org/messages/why-do-christians-preach-and-sing.

explains why one gift of the new birth is the gift of holy sight.[6] In our conversion, the Spirit not only raised a dead heart to life, but He also gave us the eyes to see and enjoy the beauty that is God. It is by seeing God as He is, in all of His holy glory, that transforms our lives.

In the third chapter of 2 Corinthians, Paul speaks to how the Spirit's work of lifting our blindness, helping us to see God (holy vision), is transformative in that it leads to godliness: "But when one turns to the Lord, the veil is removed. Now the Lord is the Spirit, and where the Spirit of the Lord is, there is freedom. And we all, with unveiled face, *beholding the glory of the Lord, are being transformed into the same image from one degree of glory to another.* For this comes from the Lord who is the Spirit" (2 Cor. 3:16–18, emphasis added). The scenario from which Paul builds his point is when Moses went up to Mount Sinai to receive from God the two tablets of stone that were inscribed with the law. After being with God for forty days and forty nights, Moses came back down the mountain, among the people, and to his surprise, his skin shone

---

[6] Adapted from Piper's quote ". . . conversion, faith, being saved, new birth, it's a gift of seeing" in "Seeing and Savoring the Supremacy of Jesus Christ Above All Things," January 1, 2012; https://www.desiringgod.org/messages/seeing-and -savoring-the-supremacy-of-jesus-christ-above-all-things.

"because he had been talking with God" (Exod. 34:29). Due to the fear of the people and their not wanting to come near Moses while his face shone with a residual glory, he placed a veil over his face, covering, if you will, this glory from the sight of the people.

In the same way, before the Spirit gives us the eyes to see, we are absolutely blind to glory, blind to the beauty of God, as we've already come to know, but in our turning to the Lord (which too is the Spirit's work of making us alive so that we can turn), the veil that covers our hearts, keeping us from seeing and delighting in that glory, is removed. One chapter over, we are told again how our *seeing* is a gift, and with this gift, we can see glory. "In their case, the god of this age has *blinded the minds of the unbelievers to keep them from seeing the light of the gospel of the glory of Christ*, who is the image of God. . . . For God who said, 'Let light shine out of darkness,' has shone in our hearts *to give the light of the knowledge of God's glory in the face of Jesus Christ*" (2 Cor. 4:4, 6, emphasis added). John Piper once said, "What's the best thing that the gospel bought for us? Forgiveness of sins, justification, eternal life—those are glorious. They're all means to the end, and *the end is* the light of the gospel of the glory of Christ, the beauty

141

of Christ, the person shining forth."[7] In other words, our being forgiven, justified, atoned for are worth our praise, but these gifts are not higher than the ultimate one, which is God Himself, to see and know Him forever. We had to be forgiven so that we can know God. We had to be justified, so that we can know God. Our sins had to be atoned for so that we can know God. This is what makes the good news good, that we were blind and now we can see . . . God.

As the Bible says, we become what we behold. It is true of idol worshipers and it is true of God's children. To repeat a passage I've already included: "And we all, with unveiled face, *beholding the glory of the Lord, are being transformed into the same image* from one degree of glory to another" (2 Cor. 3:18, emphasis added). And what exactly is this glory that we are to behold? Or, if I had to ask it another way, what is it about Jesus that by beholding it in Him, I too become like Him?

Glories to Behold

For many, the beholding begins with the glory of His love, communicated most clearly in His incarnation, crucifixion, and resurrection. "But God proves His love for

---

[7] John Piper, "The Highest Good of the Gospel," October 17, 2013; https://www.desiringgod.org/messages/the -highest-good-of-the-gospel.

us in this: While we were still sinners, Christ died for us" (Rom. 5:8). As I've said earlier, but in a different way, we are born thinking we know what love is, and at first, what we know of it isn't taught or a matter of the intellect at all but it's tangible and experienced. We come into the world with parents who love us and say so. Hearing it, we store the language in our minds, but *seeing* it shapes who we are and how we tend to understand love at all. This could be why the term itself and our love of it is so fundamental to our understanding of God and why the Spirit has to reorient, deepen, and reveal the differences between the love we've known and the love Christ has displayed.

What I mean to say is this: the love of our parents, spouses, boyfriends, girlfriends, neighbors, best friends, cousins, grannies, and grandpas don't hold a candle to the settled flame that God's love is. Every person mentioned, no matter how much they love you, their love could never save your soul. But Christ, through whom your parents, spouses, boyfriends, girlfriends, neighbors, best friends, cousins, granny, and grandpa were made, made a choice. He saw you trying to quench your thirst with broken cisterns, and He didn't let your blindness to the all-satisfying fountain of the living waters that He is keep Him from becoming like you so that He could help you. The transcendent God who exists differently from everything that has been made took on flesh, lived with it and others until on the cross, His flesh breathed its last. The burial site, a real place and also a metaphor for our state before we believe, is where His body lay before the Spirit raised Him on the third day (Rom. 8:11). It's said that timing is everything, and if I didn't know any better, I'd suppose that since Christ died then, I've missed the chance to have life now, but Christ's blood isn't held captive by time and space. For Paul, by the Spirit, to say that *"while* we were still sinners, Christ died for us"* (Rom. 5:8, emphasis added) is to say that although the substitutionary death of Christ happened before I was even born, or sinned, the application of His saving grace is just as present and available now as it was then. Glory.

Another glory to behold is Christ's peace. Before His crucifixion, Jesus told His disciples, "Peace I leave with you; *my peace* I give to you" (John 14:27, emphasis added). The peace that Jesus promises to give is the peace that He Himself has. This peace is the shalom of the heart and mind that neither shivers at what is to come nor becomes unsettled with what is already here. When you turn in your Bible to the time when Jesus calmed the sea, did your heart behold Him there? There He is, on a boat that's being tossed and turned on the wave's edge, discontent to stay in its place, when the indiscriminate water decides to fall into the ship and spread about the vessel, threatening to cover the whole thing before sundown. Everyone onboard feels the blue sea on their feet, coming close to the bottom of their knees. They run to the stern, and what do they see? Peace. Jesus is still, sleeping, at rest. Eyes closed, body tucked to keep warm while there is complete chaos above. Could this have been mere exhaustion? Raising folks from the dead and preaching to dead people are tiresome tasks, I'm sure, but anxiety cares nothing about how tired one is; it will keep you awake so as to convince you that you mustn't sleep lest you lose control. This here is the peace that is essential to a holy God.

One who knows all things and controls all things cannot and will not be troubled by what He has infinite knowledge of and complete sovereignty over. Underneath human anxiety is the reversal of identity in which the finite attempts to be infinite. With our finite knowledge, we want to know everything so as not to be caught off guard by anything. With our finite abilities, we want and try to control everything so we're not controlled by anything. We fail to do both because it's impossible to be like God in this way, making the peace of God elusive for those who need it most. But behold Jesus. He is forever settled, unshaken, and unbothered to the point that He can sleep like a baby while a storm rages war on his resting place. Being the Creator of it and thus Lord over it, He commands the storm to do what He has always had and what He is never hesitant to do, "Peace! Be still!" Glory.

Another glory worth seeing and savoring[8] is the kindness of God. His kindness is often used as an incentive, relative to His kindness toward us. "But love your enemies, and do good, and lend, expecting nothing in return, and your reward will be great, and you will be sons of the Most High, for he is kind to the ungrateful and the evil" (Luke 6:35). Christ, the kind King, doesn't walk in the kind of kindness that's born of pure sentiment and superficial "niceness." His kindness is not an elevated form of cordiality, as if His smile toward sinners was just that, a smile, and nothing more. No tender heart. No covenant commitment to do good. No authentic care for their well-being that doesn't go beyond a random act of benevolence, observable only when He feels it. No, no, no. He is rich with kindness toward those who have never deserved it. To the just and the unjust, He has given them a daily life filled to the brim with laughter between friends, love between lovers, a womb to carry a new life, food and culture and entertainment, a diversity of delights. He hasn't withheld such joys from any of Adam's children. They are available to

---

[8] The phrase "seeing and savoring" is taken from the title of John Piper's book, *Seeing and Savoring Jesus Christ* (Wheaton, IL: Crossway, 2004).

all including the ones that will never give Him their hearts in return.

As if that wasn't enough, He spent the wealth of His kindness through the sacrifice of His body. "Though he was rich, yet for your sake he became poor, so that you by his poverty might become rich" (2 Cor. 8:9). By emptying Himself to become man, He lay aside the rights and riches becoming of His deity so that in Him, by virtue of His supreme kindness, you may be rich. The prosperity being spoken of is far above the wealth related to cash and coins. It would be an unkind gesture toward us and an unfathomable thing for Christ to give His life only to secure us financially, knowing that what we were getting from His hand, the moths and rust would eventually destroy. The riches we've inherited are that of another, more lasting kind of glory. In it is "every spiritual blessing," "an inheritance" leading to "the praise of his glory" (Eph. 1:3, 11–12). We are "heirs of God" and "co-heirs with Christ" who will one day "share in his glory" (Rom. 8:17 NIV)—the glory He emptied Himself of so that we can participate in it. It was Paul who said, *"For all things are yours, whether Paul or Apollos or Cephas or the world or life or death or the present or the future—all are yours"* (1 Cor. 3:21–22, emphasis added), and our Lord who said, "He who overcomes *shall inherit all things, and I will be his God and he shall be My son"* (Rev. 21:7 NKJV, emphasis added).

If there is anything else to be said about the kindness of God, and there is always more to say, it would be how because of it, we are able to see, know, speak with, hear from, talk about, delight in, and live eternally with the holy transcendent God who created heaven and earth. Is this not the root of our regenerate joy? For what other reason have we given God our songs, poems, words, wisdom, body, mind, marriage, children, heart, and our morning's first hello if it's not bellowing up from our heart's happiness in the knowledge of Him? His kindness was given to lead us to repentance (Rom. 2:4), and it has (for those who have been born again, that is). He is the glorious One, transcendent above all but close enough to be discovered by unveiled sight. In our turning, our eyes were opened to the one-of-a-kind God, who was, and is, and is to come, and all that we have seen is infinitely better than anything we will ever see. For what have we done to deserve the turn of His cheek and the welcome of His hand? Nothing. To us we have received these things because it is God's holy nature to be as good as this. Oh the benevolent kindness of God. Glory.

These attributes we now have eyes to see, they only scratch the surface of what we might behold about God.

They only give us facets of His glory, a glory that would take all of eternity to take in. But beholding that glory, as seen in the Son, even in parts and glimpses and facets, we are transformed into His image, and as we've observed, that image is one of unhindered holiness. Notice that of the glories highlighted above—love, peace, and kindness—they are also three of the characteristics visible in the lives of those who are led by the Holy Spirit. "But the fruit of the Spirit is love, joy, peace, patience, kindness, goodness, faithfulness, gentleness, self-control" (Gal. 5:22–23). The fruit the Spirit produces in us is the very character of Jesus Himself. In Alexander MacLaren's exposition of 2 Corinthians 3, he says, "Why, if you look closely enough into a man's eye, you will see in it little pictures of what he beholds at the moment; and if our hearts are beholding Christ, Christ will be mirrored and manifested on our hearts. Our characters will show what we are looking at, and ought, in the case of Christian people, to bear His image so plainly, that men cannot but take knowledge of us that we have been with Jesus."[9] Beholding, we become.

---

[9] Alexander MacLaren's *Exposition of Holy Scripture*; https://biblehub.com/commentaries/maclaren/2_corinthians/3.htm.

Chapter 7

ᚻoly ᚻow?: Behold, We Become

AS WE'VE EXPLORED, OUR becoming like Christ is called sanctification, or as many say, "transformation." To put this in front of you again: "And we all, with unveiled face, beholding the glory of the Lord, *are being transformed into the same image* from one degree of glory to another" (2 Cor. 3:18, emphasis added). Switching languages for a second exposes the fullness of the word and how it is used in another place. What do I mean? That in the original language, transformation is the same as transfiguration. It is probable that in Paul's mind, he is connecting the transfiguration of Christ with the transformation of Christians. The metamorphosis that Jesus underwent before the three disciples was different from us in the sense of His transfiguring was His glory being unveiled. When His face "shone like the sun" and His clothes became "white as light," it was the inner glory of Christ's nature shining through the embodied flesh that concealed it (Matt. 17:2). As one commentary puts it, it is

> not that he showed his Divine nature, or laid aside his human body; his bodily nature remained in its entirety, but permeating it was an effulgence which indicated the Godhead. Perhaps it might be said, as an old writer puts it, that the Transfiguration was less a new miracle than the temporary cessation of an habitual miracle; for the veiling of his glory was the real marvel, the Divine restraint which prohibited the illumination of his sacred humanity.[1]

What the disciples beheld was the inner essence of God, the source of all divine light coming out, transforming the visual appearance of Jesus. Just as, but different from, Moses who after being with God, the appearance of Moses' face was changed, shining with a visible light. The difference is that the glory on Moses' face was a *reflected* glory. With Jesus, the transfiguration displayed His *inherent* glory.[2] So it is with any Christian who beholds the glory of the

---

[1] Joseph S. Exell, general ed., *The Pulpit Commentary*, Matthew 17 (2019, Kindle edition).

[2] R. C. Sproul, Sermon: "Transfiguration (Mark 9:2–12)," https://www.youtube.com/watch?v=rzSSdijKz_I&t=1033s.

Lord; they are only able to reflect what they have actually seen. Deeper than that, they are only able to be holy, a visible and discernible state of being, if they have been gifted with a holy nature. We can only be what we really are, and if born anew, we have an inner glory shining forth from the Spirit of the living God who is the agent of our very own transfiguration. Bright enough for the world to see. Real enough to prove that to be a Christian is to be authentic and thus display the holiness becoming of a new creature.

It's important to state that although the Spirit is the one that causes us to see, regenerating our nature, converting our souls, empowering us to walk as "children of light" (Eph. 5:8), there is yet and still an obligation on our part to participate with the Spirit in the process of sanctification. That is to say that our growing in holiness is not passive in any way. Philippians 2:12–13 speaks to the paradox that sanctification can be when it says, "Therefore, my beloved, as you have always obeyed, so now, not only as in my presence but much more in my absence, work out your own salvation with fear and trembling, for it is God who works in you, both to will and to work for his good pleasure." Once we are raised from the dead, it would be silly to assume that we can and should do nothing to grow in living as God does just as it would be foolish to think that a planted seed can grow without the soil being watered. Beholding the

Lord is fundamentally *active*. The sun in all of its radiance, shines above us on most days, but it will only be seen by those who decide to turn their faces up and look.

But where do we look? What can show us such glory that we might be changed by it? Where we look is simple, accessible, and not hidden from us. It is the Holy Scriptures that put forth a constant picture of God, as He is to be seen and understood. Inspired by the Holy Ghost, preserved by Him, and interpreted with His illuminative help too, it is there, in the pages scattered with narratives, songs, poems, and letters, that we can behold Christ. He is the glory in all of the above. The sacrificial system, the scapegoat, the blood-red doorpost, the tabernacle, and the holy place. He is the rejected brother with His Father's robe. He is the one with slingshot in hand, the savior of a timid people. He is the morning manna and evening light. He is Isaac and the ram, Jacob's ladder, and David's King. He is the serpent lifted up and the God brought low. He is the law's source and fulfillment. He is the psalmist's delight and the epistle's explanation. Someone might say that I've just taken the familiar stories of Scripture and made them be other than what they are, but truly, I'm only bearing witness to the Gospel of Luke where it says, "And beginning with Moses and all the Prophets, [Jesus] interpreted to them in all the Scriptures the things concerning himself" (Luke 24:27).

Where does Jesus go when trying to show His disciples the glory of who He is? How does He help them behold all He has fulfilled from them? Scripture. We cannot behold Him as clearly in any other place than in the Word He has given to us, and as it's read and believed, we are transformed. As Piper would put it:

> This is how God designed the Scriptures to work for human transformation and for the glory of God: the Scriptures reveal God's glory. This glory, God willing, is seen by those who read the Bible. This seeing gives rise, by God's grace, to savoring God above all things—treasuring him, hoping in him, feeling him as our greatest reward, tasting him as our all satisfying good. And this savoring *transforms* our lives.[3]

By saying that we behold God in God's Word and are thus transformed by what we see, I am not implying that just seeing is enough. There is and has always been a kind of deception among the religious that the mere reading of God's Word is sufficient in and of itself to make its readers

---

[3] John Piper, *Reading the Bible Supernaturally* (Wheaton, IL: Crossway, 2017), 141.

into godly people. That in the morning, when we open our leather-bound Bible or swipe left and right to access an app, we are changed simply by reading. God knows I wish it were as simple as that, but haven't we known (or been) those who can quote the Bible with ease while still managing to live like an embodied demon? Even they— demons, that is—know what is biblically true about God. During Jesus' earthly ministry, demons were quicker to acknowledge the validity of who Jesus was before humans did. Before begging to possess pigs, they called Him "Son of the Most High God" (Mark 5:7). The demon that made his home in a man visiting the synagogue said to Jesus, *"I know who you are—the Holy One of God!"* (Luke 4:34). James sarcastically commended the fruitless "faith" of the recipients of his letter when he wrote, "You believe that God is one; you do well. Even the demons believe—and shudder!" (James 2:19). Which says to me that a demon may very well hear Deuteronomy 6:4 quoted from his favorite pulpit, which says, "Hear, O Israel: The Lord our God, the Lord is one," and with demonic fervor say "Amen."

How we interact with what Scripture tells us distinguishes us from demons only if and when we *believe* what it is that we *see*. Demons have shown themselves to know the right facts about Jesus, but they rebel against what they know, revealing that their knowledge of God is superficial in that it may cause them to acknowledge Him but it doesn't lead them to glorify Him. Just as it was with the religious leaders in Jesus' day. They knew more than most and lived worse than them too. You'd think that being an "expert of the law" would lead to a particular holiness, birthed from all of that knowledge, but it only worked to teach them how to look holy without actually being so. They were "whitewashed tombs," a dead version of purity and light, with hearts similar to that of a cemetery, full of "dead people's bones and all sorts of impurity" (Matt. 23:27 NLT).

Beholding and Believing

When exposing their ignorance and hypocrisy, Jesus often reminded the Pharisees of their titles to show the inconsistency of knowing so much and living so unrighteous. They dedicated their lives to the study of God's Word, searching them as if they'd find eternal life in the very words themselves when, in fact, if they only believed what they knew, they'd know that eternal life was found in Christ and Christ alone. To them, Jesus said, *"You search the Scriptures because you think that in them you have eternal life; and it is they that bear witness about me, yet you refuse to come to me that you may have life"* (John 5:39–40, emphasis added). And why after searching the Scriptures did they refuse to come to this Jesus who

157

Scripture bore witness to? It's because they didn't *believe* what they *read*. "For if you *believed Moses, you would believe me*; for he wrote of me. But if *you do not believe his writings*, how will you believe my words?" (John 5:46–47, emphasis added). Beholding Christ, they did not become like Him because they did not see nor believe what was already written about Him.

There is an incredible connection between beholding and believing and how these things precede becoming. Remember when we talked about the folks who worship idols and how they look like whatever they look to? How they therefore become just as lifeless as the gods they love? Did you notice how the psalmist describes the reason for this transformation? He says, "Those who make them become like them; *so do all who trust in them*" (Ps. 115:8, emphasis added). It is not as though they are simply putting their eyes toward the idols, like a man does an attractive face or a child does an unclaimed piece of candy. No. Their eyes are a metaphor for where they've placed their faith. They look because they believe. Lovers of idols do so because they trust that the created thing can provide, satisfy, help, protect, and so on. And even if such faith is futile, it is still faith, one that transforms see-ers into the image they believe most. Their misplaced faith informs their way of life because what we believe governs how we behave.

After feeding 5,000 people a good helping of bread and fish, Jesus told the returning crowd that He was the true food. That what they ate, though satisfying for now, would not last beyond the moment. Similar to the manna their ancestors knew would rot before they woke, just in time for another meal from heaven. This bread, just like theirs, would be gone before the next morning. Against the backdrop of their once-fed, now-empty stomachs, a parable of their sometimes-full, easily emptied souls, Jesus says that He is the bread of life. If the average listener were anything like the average Bible reader, Jesus' testimony about Himself would become nothing more than a good verse to quote, an encouraging caption to have, or a wonderful tattoo to live with, but what He said about Himself wasn't intended to just be heard or seen but to be *believed* because it's in the believing where the words are experienced.

Jesus tells them who He is and continues to describe what happens when His words about Himself are treated as true: "I am the bread of life; whoever comes to me shall not hunger, and whoever believes in me shall never thirst" (John 6:35). "Whoever comes" is the same as "whoever believes." To paraphrase the Lord's words, He is saying, "Whoever believes in Me will never hunger and never thirst because they have come to Me and I have filled them."

Jesus doesn't want them or us to just have an intellectual relationship with the words themselves, but rather, that by believing, we'd bear fruit that's consistent with knowing the person who holds the title. Consider your most besetting sins and how they reveal the parts of you that are hungry or thirsty. There is a world of passions within us, waging war against our souls by tempting the eyes of our hearts to look to (trust in) everything else as a means to quench its thirst and quiet its growl. We are a needy folk, and this is nothing to be ashamed of because needlessness belongs to God and God alone. And if God has no needs, then God is completely sufficient in and of Himself, which is to say that He has endless resources that He will never need another to restore or preserve. If this is what it means for God to be bread—that He is truly able to satisfy in such a way that our hunger is replaced with fullness, our thirst quenched, too—then it is not enough to tell you to "stop sinning." Instead, I will say, "Behold Christ, He is the bread of life. Go to Him and be filled."

Believing and Becoming

How does believing that Jesus is the bread of life make the believing one holy? Continuing with the metaphor of food, bread in particular is not a light thing to eat (if it's made rightly, of course). It's heavy, dense, glutenous, and easy to stretch. Give a family bread and you have given them a food that will fill the belly quick. Once it's consumed, the stomach left with no room in it, the body is satisfied to the point that it can see another piece of bread, or meal, or money, or sexual temptation, or opportunity for the ego, and not confuse the want with need. To be satisfied is to be full. To be full is to mean that there is no more room for anything else. So then, holiness begins to characterize those who trust Christ to fill them with Himself because all their needs, in body, mind, and soul, are met in God, which sets them free from depending on anything else in heaven and earth to do the same.

The psalmist Asaph knew this to be true, which is why he said to God, "Whom have I in heaven but you? And there is nothing on earth that I desire besides you. My flesh and my heart may fail, but God is the strength of my heart and my portion forever" (Ps. 73:25–26). It is not as if the psalmist had no other desires. He, like us, was an image-bearer, and the very image He was privileged to bear was that of God, who also has the capacity to feel. Being able to feel at all finds its origin in God Himself. So our affections are not foreign, nor are they fundamentally evil. They make us humans with the power to love and be loved, weep with those who weep, enjoy our lovers and our friends. But sin's mishandling of them is what drives us to do inhumane things. When sin is intertwined with our affections, it causes conflict, lust, envy, jealousy, sexual immorality, drunkenness, sorcery, fits of anger (Gal. 5:19–21). We sin because we *feel* like it, and we sin because we *love* it. No wonder we resist the call to holiness like a bad dream because we have too many desires competing for our whole heart.

What are we to do with such sins, or desires to sin? We must dethrone them first, by way of repentance, coming to terms with their incompetence and the impossibility of them being a worthwhile love, a heavy bread. When the Spirit regenerates our hungry soul, He doesn't leave it empty like the tomb Jesus left to itself. Instead, we are given a new heart, as we now know, and with it comes an affection for God that sits enthroned above all others. Thomas Chalmers famously put it this way when he wrote, "We have already affirmed how impossible it were for the heart, by any innate elasticity of its own, to cast the world away from it; and thus reduce itself to a wilderness. The heart is not so constituted; and the only way to dispossess it of an old affection, is by the expulsive power of a new one."[4] Our love of sin is rooted in our unbelief in God and

---

[4] Thomas Chalmers, *The Expulsive Power of a New Affection* (Wheaton, IL: Crossway, 2020).

our weak affections toward Him. By weak, I am referencing C. S. Lewis when he said, "It would seem that Our Lord finds our desires not too strong, but too weak. We are half-hearted creatures, fooling about with drink and sex and ambition when infinite joy is offered us."[5] When God is believed to be bread, savior, sustainer, provider, comforter, Lord, King, and everything else He has revealed himself to be, the heart will say, "There is nothing on earth that I desire besides you." Because it has found the person that has everything the heart needs. Desiring God above all things is the soil from which holiness is grown. We are already empowered to flee sin through the Spirit, and we will *want* to and *choose* to put to death what is earthly in us when we believe God is infinitely better than everything we are tempted to leave Him for.

Beholding God's glory in God's Word and believing all that it shows you transforms you into "that same image." This language of imaging God began in Genesis when the Godhead proclaimed, "Let us make man in our image, after our likeness" (Gen. 1:26). This theme is also present throughout the Epistles, in relation to looking like Christ, being holy as He is. Romans 8:29 says, "For those whom

---

[5] C. S. Lewis, *The Weight of Glory* (New York: HarperCollins, 1949), 26.

he foreknew he also predestined to be *conformed to the image of his Son . . ."* (emphasis added). The "old self" as Paul calls it in Colossians 3, refers to the person and behaviors that shaped who we were before the Spirit made us new. Prior to our regeneration, we were as evil as the night is long, but with being made alive, we are told and miraculously able to disrobe ourselves of that ancient way of life. Instead we are clothed by the "new self" which is "being renewed in knowledge after *the image of its creator"* (Col. 3:10, emphasis added). Beholding Christ motivates us to holiness by our observing the moral purity and transcendent beauty of Jesus, but through this vision, we are also taught the way of Jesus.

> But that is not the way you learned Christ!— assuming that you have heard about him and were taught in him, as the truth is in Jesus, to put off your old self, which belongs to your former manner of life and is corrupt through deceitful desires, and to be renewed in the spirit of your minds, and to put on the new self, *created after the likeness of God in true righteousness and holiness.* (Eph. 4:20–24, emphasis added)

I would hope that we know what God looks like by now. If we don't, the world and the flesh will give us deficient ways to image Him, telling us that we can look like God and Satan at the same time. Worldliness is nothing less than the lust of the flesh, the lust of the eyes, and the pride of life (1 John 2:16); this being the very pulse of whatever context we call home, we must never take our cues from a dying thing on how to live. If we are unclear about "the truth" as told and revealed in Christ, the world will inevitably woo us back to itself. David Wells, explaining how convincing the world can be, says, "The world is that system of values whose source is human sinfulness and whose expression is cultural. It is that collective life which validates our personal sin. It is everything in society that makes sinful attitudes and practices look normal."[6] But sin will never be normal. It is and will always be offensive to God. If we behold the world and its ways more than Christ, be not surprised when you look more like it than you do Jesus.

Looking to Christ, we know what God is like. Who and how He is—this is the end goal of our "becoming." Remember God, good in every way. Set apart from

---

[6] David Wells, *God the Evangelist: How the Holy Spirit Works to Bring Men and Women to Faith* (Grand Rapids: Wm. B. Eerdmans Publishing, 1987), 115.

everything that there is, being in a class all by Himself, enthroned on high, He sits where the angels sing His praises. Let us recall and think on His holiness yet again: He is totally free to be who He is and He can never be who He is not. Nothing in heaven or on earth controls the sovereign God. This freedom is expressed in His creating us, in love. God didn't create because anything outside of Himself told Him to or convinced Him that He should. It wasn't out of need that He made the world, as if God was dependent on what He's made to be whole. No. He created the world and all that's in it because it pleased Him to bring into being creatures that would share in the love He has always had for His Son through the love-bond of the Spirit. "Father, I desire that they also, whom you have given me, may be with me where I am, to see my glory that you have given me because *you loved me before the foundation of the world*" (John 17:24, emphasis added). And "I made known to them your name, and I will continue to make it known, *that the love with which you have loved me may be in them*, and I in them" (John 17:26, emphasis added). God is self-giving in that way, to make us so that we may know Him. God's love for us in Christ, as poured out by the Spirit (Rom. 5:5), has brought us into fellowship with Him and the Son; from there, we have come to behold the beauty of His holiness, and by beholding it, we become as lovely as He is.

Looking to Christ, we too are set apart from the world and the things it delights in. To God we belong, giving Him our bodies as a living sacrifice, our mouths as His ambassadors, our feet to bring His good news. Believing God to be the all-satisfying bread of life that He is, He fills us and frees us from being enslaved to everything and everybody. Being satisfied in God makes us totally "independent of our environment" since we are no longer needy of people or circumstances to make us happy or whole.[7] As "people who are free" we are liberated to love as generously as God does, not repaying evil for evil but turning our cheek, while pursuing moral purity with all that we have. Clothed in the newness of Christ, we "put to death therefore what is

---

[7] When I speak of being independent of environment, I do not mean we do not need external things like food or water or the community of faith; rather, I draw from R. A. Torrey in his book *The Person and Work of the Holy Spirit* (2013). On page 56, when exploring the filling of the Holy Spirit, Torrey says once a person receives the Spirit, He then fills us with a well of water that is forever springing up, "satisfying us from within" regardless of circumstances like "health or sickness, prosperity or adversity." Thus, we are "independent of our environment," no longer needy of it to make us happy. In other words, the Spirit of God satisfies to such a degree that we aren't dependent on our circumstances to do so.

earthly . . . sexual immorality, impurity, passion, evil desire, and covetousness, which is idolatry" (Col. 3:5) And put on, as God's chosen ones, "holy and beloved, compassionate hearts, kindness, humility, meekness, and patience, bearing with one another . . ." (Col. 3:12–13a). This heaven-empowered love toward God and our neighbors may set us at odds with the world around us, but even then, as God's peace is, ours is too—settled and safe. It is the world that Christ has overcome, and through Christ, we will overcome it too. Of the saints, He says, "The one who conquers, I will grant him to sit with me on my throne, as I also conquered and sat down with my Father on his throne" (Rev. 3:21). And there, finally, after we have breathed our last, we will see why our dying is gain. Opening those eyes that were once blind, now seeing, He will finally appear, and do you know what will happen next? "We know that when he appears *we shall be like him, because we shall see him as he is*" (1 John 3:2, emphasis added).

Beholding, we become; holy.

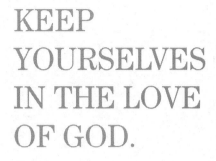

KEEP YOURSELVES IN THE LOVE OF GOD.

JUDE 1:21a

While often overlooked, the Book of Jude remains as relevant today as the time it was written. God has commanded His beloved church to do the necessary work of contending for the faith in a world of unbelief, and as we do, He will keep us from falling into the same deception.

In this 7-session study from Jackie Hill Perry, dive into themes of being called, loved, and kept, and learn how to point others to Jesus in grace and truth. We serve others well when we share the whole gospel with them, not just the parts deemed attractive by our culture.

Available wherever books are sold.

Also Available for Teen Girls!